YACHT CREWING

FERNHURST OFFSHORE

YACHT CREWING

Malcolm McKeag

photographs by Tim Hore

Fernhurst Books

First published 1984 by
Fernhurst Books, 13 Fernhurst Road, London SW6 7JN

ISBN 0 906754 14 3

Acknowledgements

The publishers wish to thank Hunter Boats Ltd who kindly loaned an HB31 for use in the photo sessions, and who offered much helpful advice. Thanks are also due to all those who agreed to appear in the photographs: Sue Fielden, Ewan McEwan (and the National Sailing Centre, Cowes, for giving him leave), Paul Whitlock, Tony Pratt and the crew of 'Loujaine'.

Permission is gratefully acknowledged to reproduce the following photographs: pages 2, 13, 37, 57, 58, 79, 84, 85, and 87 – William Payne; pages 7 and 71 – Kos. The cover photograph is by Franco Pace and the design is by Behram Kapadia.

Printed & bound in Great Britain

Composition by A & G Phototypesetters, Knaphill
Printed by Ebenezer Baylis & Son Ltd, Worcester

Contents

1 · Step on board

Offshore racing yachts come in all shapes and sizes from around 22 ft overall to over 80 ft on deck. The big boats — those over, say, 40 ft overall length — rarely take novice crews, for by the time an owner graduates to a boat of that size he has usually gathered together a nucleus of regular crew who have been with him for several boats. In the rare circumstance of a brand-new owner starting his racing career with a boat of that size, designer, yard and sailmaker will usually ensure that an experienced crew is found.

The majority of offshore racing yachts is under 40 ft, and in this big and growing fleet good crews are scarce: if you don't believe that, just watch an average class of 32-footers approaching a downwind mark in a smart breeze. The leaders will drop their spinnakers cleanly and round neatly, but towards the back of the fleet the sail handling becomes more messy until, sooner or later, there comes the real drama that gives the photographers their hairy pictures.

So this book is intended to help the crew members — especially new crew members — who find themselves on that size of boat and who want to know why the slick crews can change sails without anyone noticing, while our sail changes seem to take four people on the foredeck half-an-hour (and that's without anything going wrong), and why *their* spinnakers blossom forth at the windward mark like flowers in summer while *we're* lucky to get ours up with time to spare for a beer before it has to come off again.

Differences from dinghy sailing

The basic difference between big boats and dinghies is their size (much of this book is concerned with stating the obvious — but it is only obvious when you stop to think about it). In a dinghy the two sailors have to divide the work between them: the helmsman not only steers, but also trims the mainsail, hauls the spinnaker halyard, adjusts the kicker (often, on a big boat, called the vang). The crew not merely holds the jibsheet, but watches the opposition, helps with or even calls the tactics, times the start, sets the spinnaker and takes the blame.

On a big boat there will be a number of people to split these tasks between them (a 22-footer will usually sail with four, a 27-footer with five, a 33-footer with six or seven; a 40-footer, about the biggest we are likely to deal with here, will have nine or ten; a 50-footer thirteen or fourteen, and the biggest IOR racers, the maxis, between twenty and twenty-four).

The crew members will then have more specifically defined tasks, and need not concern themselves too greatly with others: indeed the bowman is well advised to keep his tactical opinions to himself, lest That Lot Back Aft find something to complain about during his next spinnaker peel.

That does not mean the boat should be sailed by two people plus a gang of unthinking automatons: the best boats are sailed by a cohesive team where everyone thinks about the race and where very few direct orders have to be given, because everyone instinctively knows what to do. It does mean, however, that it is best to master the mechanics of big-boat sailing before trying to take over the management. If you are that good, your advice will be sought soon enough.

The bigger boat's size also requires a completely new approach to handling sails. Even on a 27-footer, the spinnaker will be powerful enough to lift a man off the deck, so guile as well as brute strength is required to handle the sails. The principal tool in this is the winch (see chapter 2), which is used to handle just about every piece of line on a big boat. On smaller yachts, some lines such as the main outhaul will be

CONTAINER

on multipart tackles, but the winch is still paramount. The new big-boat crew soon learns that his or her own strength is puny in comparison with the strength of the boat, and a new respect quickly dawns for the power of the wind in a sail.

Another major difference between dinghy sailing and big-boat sailing is the sporadic nature of the crewing job. In a dinghy, crewing is a continuing process, even if only leaning out, moving in, leaning out . . . In a big boat, there are long periods where the sailing of the boat requires the immediate attention of only three or four of the crew: helmsman, navigator, main trimmer and genoa trimmer. The remainder of the crew sit where their weight does most good, usually on the weather rail with their feet over the side.

Then comes a manoeuvre as simple as tacking or as complex as a gybe and spinnaker set, when a multitude of jobs have to be done in the shortest possible time.

BELOW *Many deck items such as spinnaker poles must be kept in designated stowages when not in use.* PREVIOUS PAGE *Crew members not actually engaged in sailing the yacht sit on the weather rail.*

Longer races

Not all races for offshore yachts are held offshore, but even a round-the-cans race for big boats normally lasts longer than a dinghy race. Twenty miles is a normal race for a small offshore boat, a short race for a big one — but even at six knots that is just over three hours, and if the breeze fails you might be out there for twice that time, or more. Offshore races tend to be between 60 and 200 miles and may involve two nights at sea.

This extra time at sea means many things. Since the weather is seldom constant for more than a few hours, sails must be changed to suit the changing conditions. It is necessary to eat on board, and to sleep. Eating, sleeping and staying warm and dry are much more important on a big boat than in a dinghy. Most of us can put up with an hour or two's discomfort during a dinghy race, but becoming cold and wet at the start of a thirty-hour race is not only very unpleasant, but also reduces your own efficiency and, if things get really bad, may distract the attention of other crew members who have to look after you.

Rules and regulations

Although rules and regulations governing the race are primarily the concern of That Lot Back Aft — the owner, skipper and navigator — there are some which directly concern the way the yacht is crewed during the race.

Handicapping systems

Virtually all offshore racing is done under some form of handicap system. The purpose of handicapping is to allow yachts of differing size and shape to race together and to allow comparison of their race times on some sort of common basis.

Elapsed time and corrected time. The handicapping system applies a mathematical calculation to the actual time the yacht takes to complete the course, to convert it into the handicap time. To distinguish the two, the time the yacht actually takes for the race (measured from the time the race started — irrespective of when she actually crossed the start line — to the moment she crossed the finish line) is called the *elapsed time*. The time that is derived after the handicapping calculation has been done is called the *corrected time*.

It is the corrected times which are compared to find the winner of the race — the yacht with the lowest corrected time wins. Apart from establishing record times for a particular course — for example the Fastnet course, the Bermuda race or the Sydney-Hobart race — elapsed times are of no great interest in offshore handicap racing, it being in the nature of things that big boats go faster than little ones, which is why we have handicapping in the first place.

Performance systems. The simplest systems are those which use observed performance information about the yachts to compare their results. If yacht A on average always completes the course 10 per cent faster than yacht B, then by adding 10 per cent to her elapsed time for a given day, and comparing it to yacht B's time for the same course on the same day, we can tell if on that day she sailed better or worse than yacht B. Few performance handicap systems are quite that crude, but it can be seen that the more times a yacht's performance has been observed the easier it is to fit her into the system. Performance handicapping systems are often used for local club racing, but their principal disadvantages are that (a) they tend not to cope well with unknown yachts, and (b) it is difficult to avoid handicapping the crew, as well as the yacht. Who is to say how much of yacht A's 10 per cent advantage is due to her size and shape and how much to the fact that she is better sailed than yacht B?

Rating systems. To overcome these disadvantages, rating systems were invented. A rating system tries to analyse mathematically the size and shape of differing yachts and reduce them all to a common denominator. All other things being equal a long yacht is faster than a short yacht, so most rating systems express this common denominator as a notional length for the yacht — and that notional length, expressed in feet, is her rating. The rating system — or rule, as it is usually known — hopes to quantify the speed potential of the yacht and, by measuring all yachts the same way, hopes to permit direct comparisons of the speed potential of differing yachts by way of their rating: a 22 ft rating yacht being adjudged to be faster than a 20 ft rating yacht, and so on.

The IOR. The most widely used rating rule in offshore racing today is the International Offshore Rule — called, for short, the IOR. We need not concern ourselves much with how it works out the rating, save to note that a fundamental problem with all rating rules is that, as soon as they are published, clever designers try to design yachts that out-smart the rule. They do this by paying particular attention to the measurements the rule takes to establish the rating, trying to increase those which will give a low rating, and trying to decrease, or at least disguise, those which give a high rating.

The IOR also lays down certain things which may and must not be done to the yacht when she is racing, and these are especially important for the crew to know about. We will look at those in a moment.

The rating itself does not tell us by how much or how little one yacht must beat another to win the race. To know that, we must know the *time allowance* one yacht gives to another, and the rating is used to establish this. There are two ways to apply time allowance: time on distance and time on time.

Time on distance. In America, particularly, time on distance handicapping is used. Here, the handicapper says (to use a crude example), if a 20 ft rating yacht can do 10 miles in 60 minutes, a 22 ft rating yacht should be able to do the same 10 miles in (say) 58 minutes — a difference in this example of 12 seconds per mile. Thus in a 50-mile race the 22-footer would be required to give the 20-footer a time allowance of 600 seconds. An obvious disadvantage of this sytem is that it ignores the effect of weather conditions: the time allowance is the same whether it is blowing a gale and the two yachts do the distance in record time, or whether it is flat calm and the two yachts take all day. A further disadvantage is that it is actually quite difficult to establish how much distance a yacht race will cover, especially if there is much beating. The distance between the marks is easy enough, but working upwind the yachts cover much more than that distance — and if, as is not uncommon in long races, the wind shifts to give one yacht a fetch where the other had a beat, the fairness of the system goes out the window.

Time on time. In British and European waters, time on time handicapping is more favoured. Here the system says that if yacht A takes 1 hour to cover a given distance, yacht B, rating lower, should cover the same distance in the same conditions in 1 hour and 1 minute — and her time allowance is expressed as 1 minute per hour. Thus if the race takes yacht A three hours, yacht B must take less than 3 hours 3 minutes; but if the race drags on for 6 hours, yacht B will have a time allowance of 6 minutes. This method has the advantage that it does not require the handicapper to predict the direction or strength of the wind when setting the handicaps, but the disadvantage that the lighter the wind and the slower the race, the better the time allowance given to the smaller boats. This can cut both ways, but usually works to the smaller boats' advantage if there is so little wind that the big boats cannot develop their full speed.

The IOR and you

The IOR is more than just a rating rule that influences the design of the yacht. So that the yacht always remains in the same trim as she was when first measured and rated, the rule is very strict about what may or may not be moved around on board while racing. Some items may not be moved at all: some items must always be kept in designated stowage areas (which must be clearly marked inside the yacht) unless the item is in use; and some items may be kept where you please, but must only be moved around if they are actually in use. Among the items which may not be moved at all are:

- the fuel and water tanks
- the batteries
- any ballast which the yacht carries
- the engine (even if you have a big enough spanner).

Items which must be kept in their marked stowage position unless actually in use include:

- the anchor
- the chain
- the spinnaker pole, if normally stowed on deck forward of the mast.

Virtually every other item carried on board must be kept in its usual stowage unless actually being put to use. This includes the sails, the toolbox, the crates of beer, portable water containers and the liferaft. In particular, although the crew may move from side to side as the yacht tacks, they are not allowed to move anything else across the boat to act as extra ballast. To do so is to cheat, but unhappily not all crew members realise this.

Sitting out. The IOR also prohibits crew members — apart from in exceptional circumstances — sitting or working outside the lifelines or guardlines. For the purpose of this rule feet and legs are disregarded — hence the practice of sitting with legs and feet over the side — but it is important to remember that your head must be inside the guardrails too. Several attempts have been made to have this rule relaxed but, at the time of writing, none has succeeded. Although some sailors point out it is more comfortable on a heeling yacht to tuck one's head under the top rail, the fear is that a person in this position would be trapped and held under water if the yacht were suddenly caught aback, or if she did an involuntary tack.

2 · Basic skills and equipment

It is sometimes said of modern racing yachts — as a criticism, not as a compliment — that the easiest way to immobilise them is to throw all the winch handles overboard. Unhappily (from a safety point of view) there is a great deal of truth in the criticism, but it points up the importance of the winch to just about every crewing task on board.

The end of the line — be it sheet, guy or halyard — which comes off the winch is known as the tail: hauling on this is called tailing and the crew whose job it is is called the tailer. By keeping a load both on the working end of the line (in other words, the pull of the sail) and a load on the tail, the turns on the winch are kept tight and friction stops the turns slipping round the barrel or drum of the winch. A toothed ratchet inside the drum prevents the drum itself from turning. If, even pulling hard on the tail, the pull of the sail causes the turns to slip, one or two extra turns will give the line more grip on the winch and allow the line to be held.

Thus the winch allows the crew to hold (snub) a heavy load, or by turning the winch drum with the handle, to haul in a much greater load than even the strongest man could budge. Using the deceptive simplicity of the sheet winch, a girl weighing 100 lb can easily control a spinnaker exerting enough pull to haul a 10-ton yacht along.

Mechanical advantage. The mechanical advantage which gives winches their power is provided either by the handle alone or by combining the power of the handle with gearing in the winch. Modern racing yachts over about 28 ft usually have winches that incorporate gears, giving two or even three speeds and thus doubling or tripling the mechanical advantage: on a big winch the power ratio available might be as much as 65:1. Such is the power of the modern winch; and such is the need, therefore, to avoid dropping the winch handles over the side.

Single-speed winch

The simplest form of winch. A toothed wheel (ratchet) inside the winch working against spring-loaded teeth (pawls) allows the barrel to turn one way but not the other. Most modern winches turn clockwise, but changing the ratchet will reverse the working direction of the winch: this is sometimes done for a particular reason or specialist application. It was once fashionable to 'hand' the winches, so that those on the port side worked the opposite way to those on the

BELOW Working as a pair — tailing and winding — to trim a sheet.

starboard side. Fortunately this is rarely found nowadays, but you might come across it on an older yacht.

Some single-speed winches have a second ratchet on the top, to allow the handle to be turned back, freewheeling, to give a more convenient pull. These are called single-speed ratchet winches. Alternatively the ratchet may be in the handle itself (see below).

Two-speed winch

On a two-speed winch, turning the handle one way — normally clockwise — turns the drum at the same rate as the handle. Turning the handle the other way turns the drum more slowly, due to gearing inside the winch, and gives more mechanical advantage — just how much more depends on the gear ratios.

Three-speed winch

Extra gearing inside the winch allows either direct winding — like a single-speed winch — or one of two lower gears to be used. The gears can be selected with a button on the top of the winch and are so arranged that turning the handle one way (normally clockwise) gives direct gear, reversing direction gives second gear and reversing direction again gives third gear. On most three-speed winches the gear-changing sequence, once begun, is automatic so the button has to be set only once — at the beginning of the tack, for example.

The advantage of multi-speed winches is not just in the greater power they give but also in the greater control they give when fine-trimming the sails, in particular the genoa.

Handles

Without the handle, the most powerful winch can be used only to snub a line that is to be held — it cannot be used to haul in the line. Handles are also expensive. So never leave a handle unattended in the winch: a stray line may catch it and flick the handle into the water, or cause some other foul-up.

Older winches had a slot in the top into which the

RIGHT This photograph gives a good view of the layout of 'Panda's' winches.

K·25
K·2
PANDA
RORC

handle, a flat bar, fitted. Most modern winches have a star-shaped hole in the top of the winch into which the star-shaped head of the handle is fitted: the majority of winch manufacturers have standardised the size and shape of the hole, so that handles can be interchangeable.

Simple handle. This just has the star head, and is merely a lever to turn the winch drum.

Ratchet handles. These have a ratchet contained in the star head, so that the handle, having turned the drum, can be pulled back half-a-turn (or just an inch or two) to give a more convenient pull (or push).

Locking handles. These have a small, turnable plate on the bottom of the star head which mates with a groove in the bottom of the hole on the winch head, locking the handle in position. The locking plate is turned by a little thumb lever on the top of the arm of the handle.

Crossed-linked winches

These are found on bigger, older boats. They were popular in the early seventies, but advances in geared winches since then have made cross-linking redundant. Elaborate under-deck gearing and linking shafts allow the winch on one side to be turned by the winch on the other side, as well as by its own handle. Additionally, handles can be put into small winding points — called anthills — on deck, out of the way of the winch itself, and the winch turned from there. The theory is that three or four people can wind one winch; in practice so much power is lost by friction that cross-linking is more trouble than it's worth, but boats built when it was popular will still have the system.

Coffee-grinders

These are the most powerful yacht winches, used mainly on yachts over 50 ft. The handles, worked by two or four people, are mounted amidships on a central pedestal and turned vertically, like bicycle pedals. Gears are used to connect the grinders to whichever winch needs to be turned.

Halyard winch

A special winch used for wire halyards, held captive on the winch. The winch barrel has two sections: one part holds all the wire save the last couple of turns, and these are taken on the second part of the spindle. Thus the loaded wire bears on the metal of the spindle and does not bite down through the turns of wire beneath it, jamming solid and causing much difficulty and bad language when the time comes to lower the sail.

Self-tailing winch

Often used for runner tails on fractional-rig boats, as well as for sheet winches on cruising boats, the self-tailer has a device on the top consisting of a metal guide bar and a wide groove round the top of the winch. The tail is turned on the drum in the usual way and then led over the guide and into the groove, where it is held by friction and a series of ridges. As its name suggests, the self-tailer allows one person only to operate the winch, using both hands for the handle while the tail is automatically fed into — and out of — the groove in the top.

Cross winching

Usually, the starboard sheet winch is used for the starboard sheet and the port winch for the port sheet, but if designer and builder have sited the winches to permit it, the starboard sheet can be led across the boat to the port winch, and vice versa. This is very useful on small boats where the last place we want the crew to sit on the beat is down to leeward. With cross-winching all the crew can be up to weather and the genoa sheet can be tended constantly without anyone having to move off the weather deck.

Riding turns

Normally, the turns on the winch lie one below the other, the line coming on at the lowest turn, round and round the winch and coming off to the tail from the uppermost turn. Occasionally, a lower turn traps over an upper turn — the cause is either a bad lead to the winch, or the winch turning too fast for the speed at which line is being pulled off, allowing the turns on

TOP, LEFT A self-tailing winch. TOP, RIGHT Using a coffee-grinder. ABOVE Joining a coffee-grinder without missing a beat. Put your hands on the other's shoulders, slide them down the arms and onto the handles.

ABOVE *A riding turn. It can only be removed by taking the load off the line.* BELOW *Basic winching (see text). The line is made off on a cleat.*

the winch to go slack. When this happens, the result is a riding turn (or turns) and the line on the winch locks up solid and cannot be taken off at the top. Worse, the turns on the winch cannot be slackened to allow the line to be paid out. If the line is a genoa sheet, this means that the yacht cannot be tacked until the riding turn is freed, or the sheet cut.

The only way to free a riding turn is take the load off the working end of the line, allowing the turns to be freed from the bottom up. On a small sail it might be possible to do this by hand, but usually it is necessary to rig another sheet — the change sheet. Attach this either to the sail at the clew, or to the working sheet using a rolling hitch. Lead the change sheet through a conveniently sited block or rig one quickly using a snap-shackle block or a snatch block. Finally take the change sheet to a spare winch (the spinnaker winch on the same side, or across the boat to another winch).

Once the weight is off the working sheet, the slack thus gained can be worked back and through the turns on the winch until the jam-up is reached and the turn under the riding turn pulled free. *Mind your fingers.*

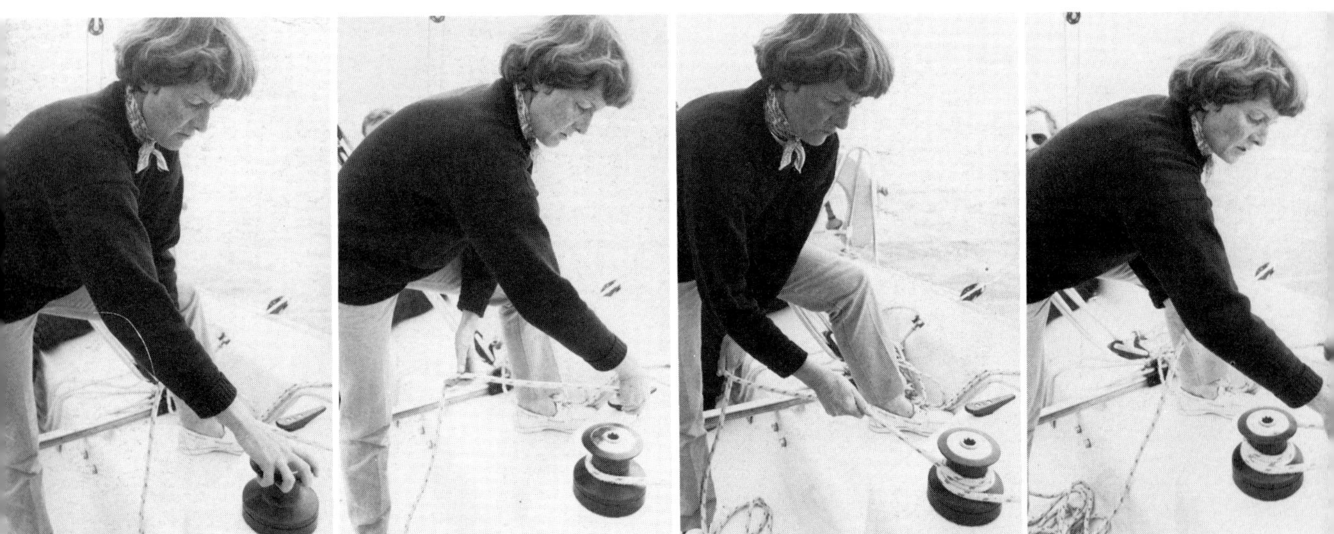

How to use a winch

Golden Rule number one is **always use a winch**. The dinghy sailor or small keelboat sailor going aboard a bigger racing boat for the first time might be tempted to take a halyard or sheet in hand, especially — with a blooper, for example — if the sail it is attached to looks small and innocent when on deck, or if the weather is light. One brief puff of wind, the sail filling unexpectedly and nastily rope-burned hands are the result. Always use a winch.

Loading the winch

Ensure that the lead of the line to the winch is correct and that the line does not snag anything — the top of the cockpit coaming, for example — or that it has not been led the wrong side of a stanchion. The line should rise to the winch at a shallow angle, so that it lands on the sloping shoulders at the lower end of the drum. If the line comes to the winch horizontally or, worse, at a slight downwards angle, riding turns will inevitably result: there must be no tendency for the line to ride up over turns already on the drum.

The winch will only turn one way, usually clockwise: if in any doubt, give the winch a spin before putting on the turns, then put the turns on the same way the winch spins. Just how many turns are needed depends on what is to be done: a heavy job will need more turns than a light job, but three turns usually give enough grip for most jobs, without having so much line on the winch that fast-hauling becomes difficult. The more turns there are, the more difficult it becomes to haul the line off quickly, and the more likely a riding turn.

Extra turns

Often — when tacking, for example — it is best to have only two or maybe three turns for the light part of the job, then put on an extra turn when the real weight comes on. This is best done with the handle — which may have been used to wind in the sheet so far gathered — removed. The important things are to keep the weight on the line already on the winch, so that the turns already on do not slip, and to ensure that your fingers are never on the inside of the extra turn where they could be trapped.

Keep the pull on the tail with the left hand, far

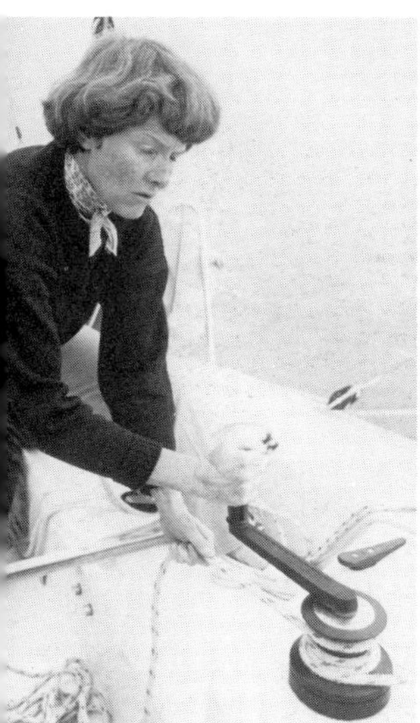

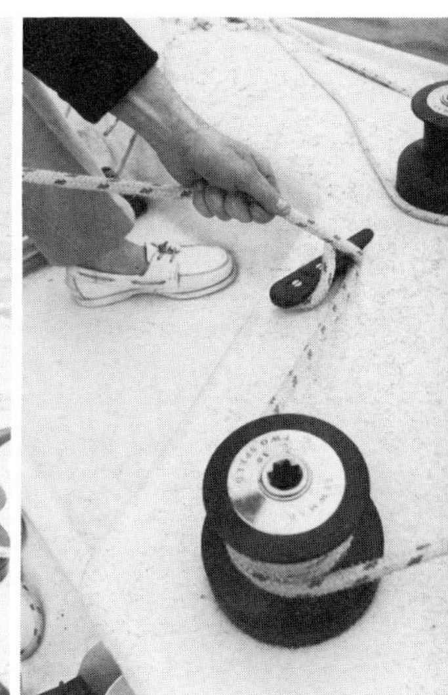

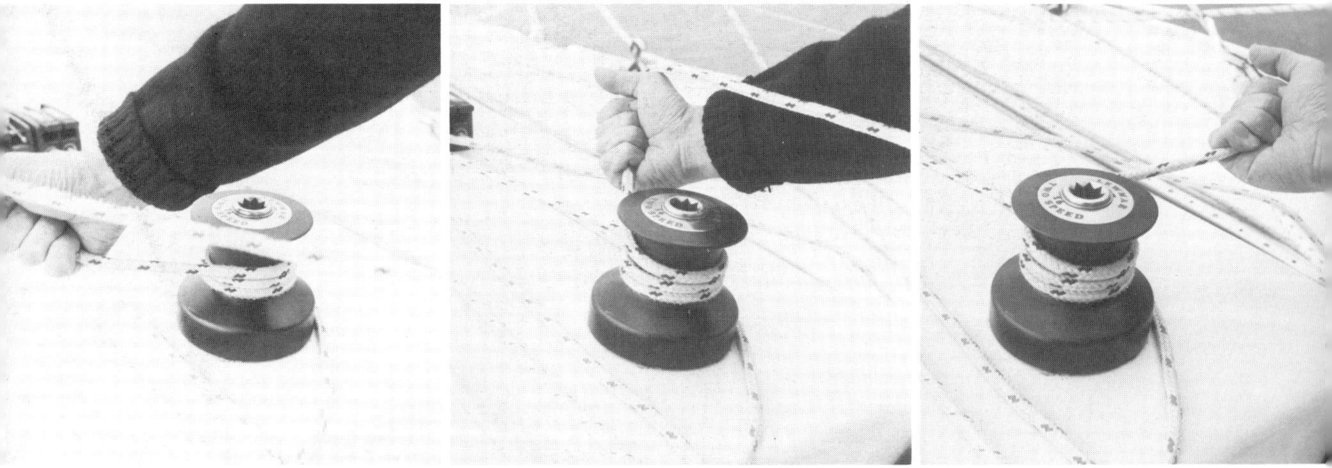

ABOVE Taking an extra turn on a winch; the fingers are kept well clear.

enough from the winch to allow the whole new turn to go on without having to move your left hand on the rope. Reverse the grip of the right hand. Now use the right hand to push the line onto the winch, moving the line round the winch at the same time (see photo sequence above). When your hand is on the opposite side of the winch, twist your wrist slightly to allow the line to go on the winch without your hand or fingers being on the inside. By now all the load is taken by the right hand, always pulling the line onto the winch. Throughout, the fingers of the right hand — the hand nearest the winch — have been on the outside of the line as it goes onto the winch.

Trimming on the winch

With a powerful winch it is possible for just one person to wind in the sheet of an already set sail so smoothly that minute adjustments to sheet tension can be made. (If this is not so, the boat is underwinched — but as a recently joined member of the crew, forbear from mentioning it to the owner at this stage.)

To ease the sheet, tail with the left hand and use the palm of the right hand flat against the turns on the drum; first to press the turns against the drum as you ease the weight off the tail, then to ease the turns round the drum so the sheet eases gently. This way, you have precise control over how much sheet is eased rather than just letting the thing go, when it will hold on the winch and then suddenly jerk out several inches.

Other hardware

The other principal item, which the crew uses all the time is the block — what the layman and the ironmonger call a pulley.

Blocks are used for a galaxy of tasks on board: rigged together they provide a tackle to give mechanical advantage (the most obvious example being the mainsheet), used singly they alter the run of a line either to avoid chafe or to give a fair lead.

The position of some blocks is fixed, but most are movable and some blocks are positioned only temporarily, for a specific task.

Lead blocks

A lead block is any block whose job it is to give a lead to a line, either round a corner or, for example, onto a winch. Lead blocks may be fairly permanently

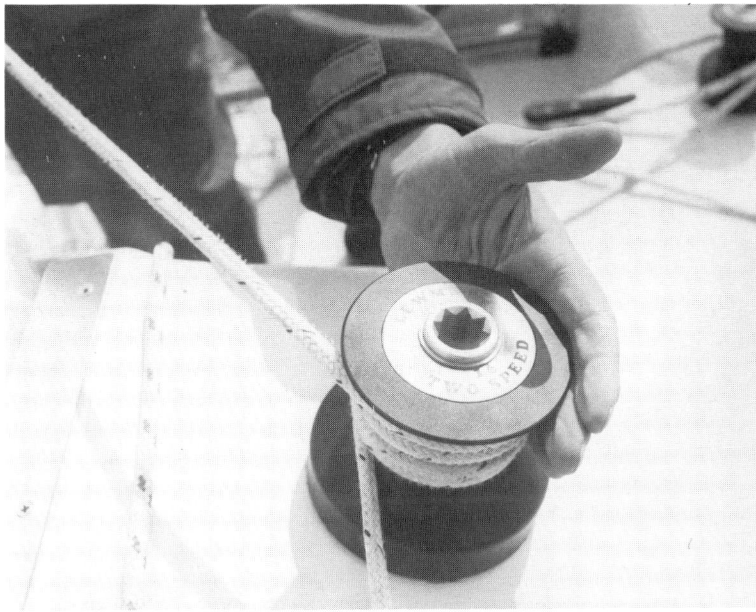

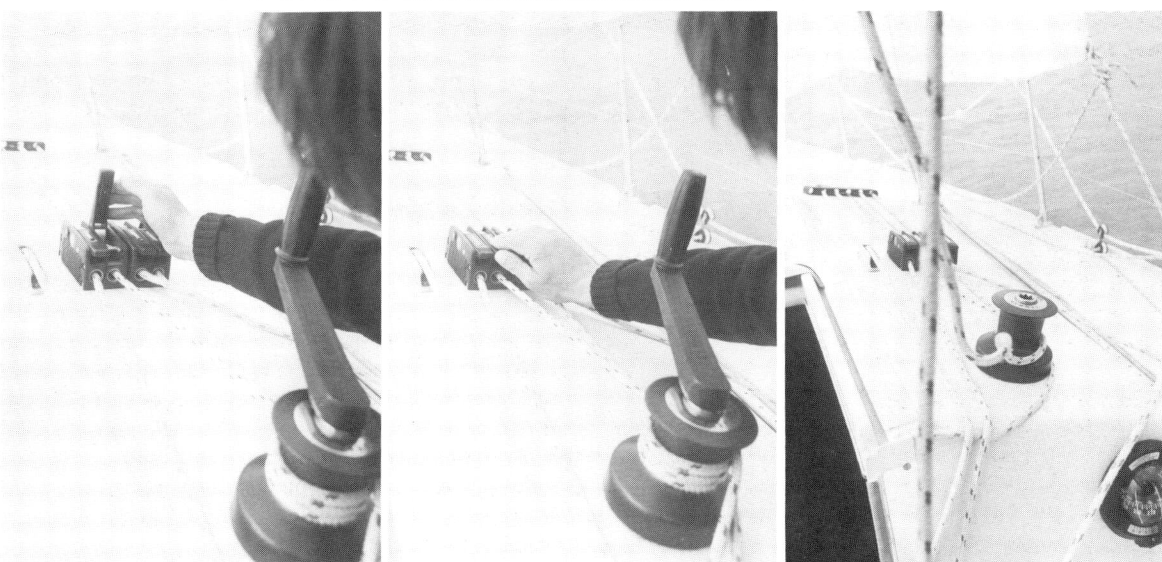

TOP Easing a line around a winch.

BOTTOM Using a stopper. Engage the stopper with the tension on; ease the line to make sure the stopper has engaged; take the handle out and the turns off.

positioned, secured to toe rail or deck eye with a shackle, or movable, secured usually with a snap shackle on a swivel.

The most obvious movable lead blocks are the *sheet leads*. These are usually mounted on metal sliders (sometimes with roller bearings and called cars) to run on tracks. They can be moved either by hand (fixed in position by a plunger which fits into a hole in the track) or by lines led through fixed blocks at each end of the track and thence to a winch. Spinnaker sheet and guy lead blocks, for example, are moved freely up and down the toe rail to give the required trim to the sail.

Snatch blocks

A very versatile block is the snatch block. This block is hinged at its swivel end to allow one of the cheeks (sides) to open, permitting the block to be fitted onto a fixed line rather than having to feed the line through the block in the usual manner. This is a very useful facility, and the snatch block is greatly used in spinnaker work, especially on larger boats.

Handy-billy

A handy-billy is just two blocks and a length of line, rove together to make a simple tackle, usually with a 2:1 purchase. The blocks have shackles, preferably snap shackles, to allow them to be clipped to suitable eyes, hooks or whatever. One of the blocks, the one that has the running end of the line, ideally has a cam cleat attached. The handy-billy can be rigged as a quick purchase to take a temporary load, hooked to main boom and toe rail to prevent the main gybing, or used as a temporary sheet to free a riding turn — in fact for a hundred and one quick jobs about the boat. It is a very seamanlike tool to have available.

BELOW *Loading a snatch block on the toe rail.*

3 · Hoisting and changing headsails

Changing headsails is the fundamental crewing task on the modern cruiser-racer. Headsails have to be changed for a variety of reasons: a change in the wind strength requires a bigger or smaller sail; a change of course requires a different sort of headsail (from the heavy number one we used on the beat, say, to the high-clewed reacher we will use on the ensuing close reach); or even a change in the sea state — coming out from the lee of the land, the waves become bigger but the breeze does not increase and the skipper may decide on a fuller headsail to give more speed and power to cope with the seas.

In an effort to keep down the cost of racing, many one-design offshore racers limit the number of sails which may be carried: so many headsails, so many spinnakers and so on. Organising clubs also have similar rules and so too does the IOR, but there are still quite a number to choose from.

Sail stowage

Before the race all these headsails will be dragged from their usual marina-stowage up in the fo'c's'le and laid in their bags on the sole of the saloon, on the lower berths and, if the boat is big enough, down beside the quarter berths too. On a well-organised boat (and over a season, it is the well-organised boats that do most of the winning) there is a carefully thought-out stowage plan. At the least, there is a list of all the sails on board posted prominently on the bulkhead, detailing the sail, what bag or sausage it is in, what wind strengths it can be carried in and where it is stowed while racing; but the very best system is the one which uses big, clear labels actually over the place where the sail is lying. So, on the port-side inner slope of the coach roof, for instance, you may find a plate proclaiming

HEAVY NUMBER ONE
NUMBER THREE
HALF OUNCE TRI
·75 RADIAL

Where each sail is kept depends on the size of boat and number of sails: but in general the sails most often used should be easiest to reach, the heaviest

---

Sails you may meet

Headsails (attached to forestay)
Drifter
No 1 genoa
No 2 genoa
No 3 genoa
No 4 genoa (sometimes called 'working jib')
Jib top (high-clewed reaching sail)

Staysails
(Smaller sails used in front of mast, but set flying)

Mainsail

Spinnakers
Crosscut
Starcut
Radial
Triradial
Floater
Flanker (flat spinnaker for reaching)
Storm spinnaker
0.5 oz, 0.75 oz . . . etc.

Blooper (or 'big boy')

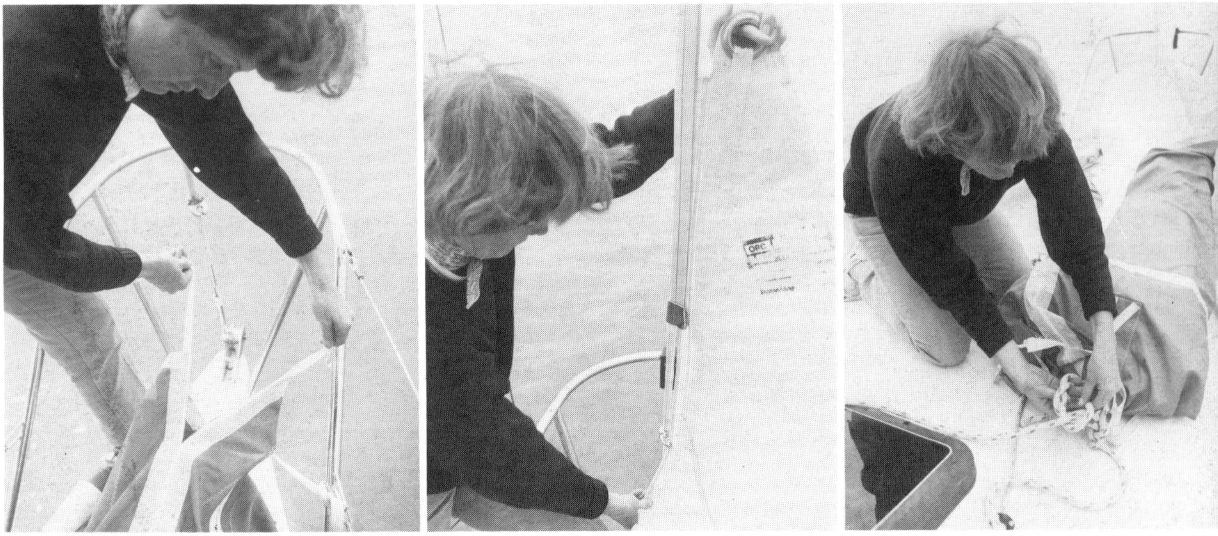

ABOVE *Basic foresail hoisting. (1) Secure the bag and partly open it; (2) feed the bolt rope through the pre-feeder and into the*

sails should be in the middle, and sails adjacent in size or in order of use should not be stowed beside each other, to reduce the chance of the wrong sail being grabbed in a panic.

Hoisting the headsail

So now we have the sail on deck. Let us assume we have not yet started, and this is our first sail-set on board this yacht.

Most racing sails are now kept in some sort of flat bag or sausage. The major sailmakers have their own ideas about what is a good system, but in general the sail will be in a sausage which has a full-length zip. Ideally, this will be a fly-away zip and the sail can be folded so that the clew ring is at one end of the sausage, the luff with its head and tack rings at the other. It is thus possible to bend on the sheets and attach the tack before undoing the zip; with the zip partly open, the halyard can be bent on, the luff tape fed into the feeder ring and up into the groove and the whole sail kept secure and tight in the sausage until the moment to hoist. Then the zip is opened, the sausage skin peels away from the sail and up she goes (and if the sausage skin has not been tied to something, it goes over the side; you only make this mistake once). It is vital to check that the sausage can open right up before bending on the sheet: some sailmakers do not favour the system just described, and fit closed-end zips. With these, the clew ring must be brought out of the zipper before the sheet is bent on.

There are two ways in which the luff of the headsail may be attached to the forestay: by hanks or in a luff groove. For normal inshore and offshore racing a headfoil with luff grooves is almost universally used, but hanks are used on some older classes.

Increasingly, all but the biggest yachts make do with three fore halyards. But for simplicity let us assume that our yacht has a headfoil (with two side-by-side luff grooves), two tack hooks and four halyards — two headsail halyards and two spinnaker halyards. On very rare occasions it will be possible to predict what the next change will be and which tack the yacht will be on when we make it, and this rarity might influence our choice of halyard and groove. But normally we will begin on the starboard halyard,

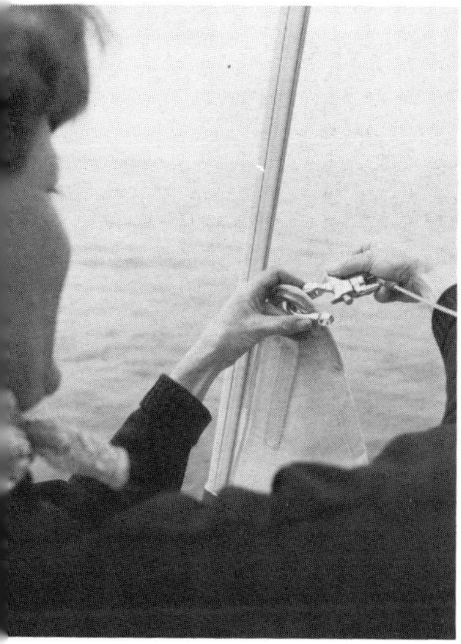

headfoil; (3) bend on the sheets. (4) Attach the halyard, (5) pull off the bag and (6) haul at the mast to help the wincher.

with the tack on the starboard hook and the sail in the starboard groove.

Having attached the sheets to the clew, attach the tack of the sail to the tack hook. Next follow along the luff tape with thumb and forefinger to make sure the sail is not twisted: this is very important, and if it becomes a matter of unvaried habit with every sail you handle, you will never have the embarrassment of that ultimate cry of foredeck failure: "Hold it — bring it down again!"

Having made sure the sail is not twisted, feed the head of the luff tape through the D-ring feeder, into the groove and attach the starboard halyard. Golden Rule Number Two: **never attach a halyard without checking aloft to see the halyard runs clear from the sheave to the sail**. (At this stage all the other halyards will probably be clipped to their stowage hooks at the mast at deck level.)

At last the sail is ready to hoist. On very big boats the foredeck hand stays up forward to see the sail aloft and the mast hand hauls on the halyard at the mast, while the tailer winds the halyard winch. On smaller boats the foredeck hand does the mast as well.

BELOW Before hoisting any sail check aloft to make sure the halyard runs clear.

Changing the headsail

There are three normal ways of changing the headsail: the bare-headed change, the side-by-side change and the tack change.

Bare-headed change

The bare-headed change is the least complicated, the least slick but not necessarily the slowest. The new sail is made ready, the old sail dropped, and the halyard changed to the new sail which is then hoisted. Of course there is a brief moment when the yacht sails bare-headed (without her headsail — hence the name) and thus rather slowly, but do not dismiss this method from the crewing repertoire. There are times when it is no slower and often quicker than struggling with a fancy change that has gone wrong. At night, in the rain, when it's blowing, with one wet sail sticking to the other and two people on the foredeck for minutes struggling and exhausting themselves, only to find the halyards have been crossed, the crew boss might well wish he'd called a bare-headed change and had the yacht going again ten minutes earlier. Another time when the bare-headed change is frequently best of all is in very light, ghosting weather. With the yacht just creeping along, minimal disturbance and crew movement is paramount and she will lose very little with a bare-headed change done quickly and gently.

Side-by-side change

In a side-by-side change the new sail goes up alongside the old sail, inside or outside depending on which halyard is in use. The yacht stays on the same tack throughout and the old sail comes down alongside the new sail.

The problem is either hoisting the new sail, or lowering the old sail, or both. Which side the new sail goes up depends on which halyard is already holding up the current sail. If the old sail is on the starboard halyard, and the yacht is on starboard tack, the new sail will have to use the port halyard and groove and thus be fed out under the old sail, dragged aloft between it and the guardrail and sheeted home. Then the old sail can be dropped inside the belly of the new sail — this is an outside hoist/inside drop. With an inside hoist/outside drop the reverse procedure is used. In either case a new sheet, called the *change sheet*, must be rove and bent on to the new sail: usually it will be rove through the spare car, placed in the correct sheeting position for the new sail. With a capful of wind in the sails, and especially if the sails are wet, the drag caused by skin friction between the two can be enormous and even two people tugging on the luff tape will not be enough to budge the wretched thing. The conversation then runs (to the person on the winch): "I pray you, friend — let the jolly halyard go."

"With all my heart I assure you, friend, I have let the halyard go this long time — pray pull a little harder . . . "

One trick is to lift the skirt of the inside sail, if that is the one to come down, to let air up between the two to effect separation, or the old clew can be brought forward to achieve the same end. This sticking problem can be really troublesome, and much time can be lost with the yacht plugging along with her bows and her speed well down.

ABOVE *Gaining extra purchase on a halyard led along the deck.*

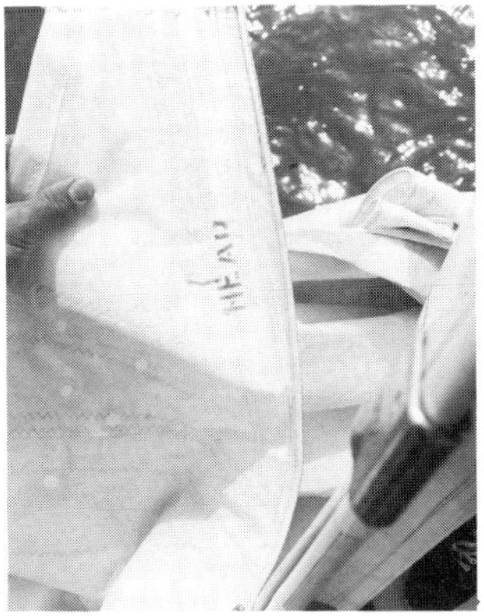

1

2

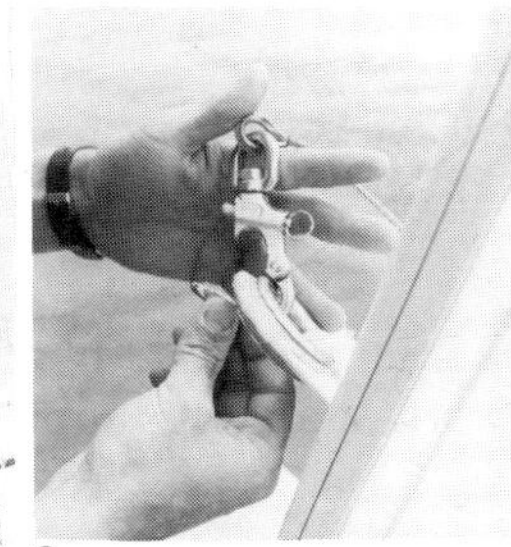

3

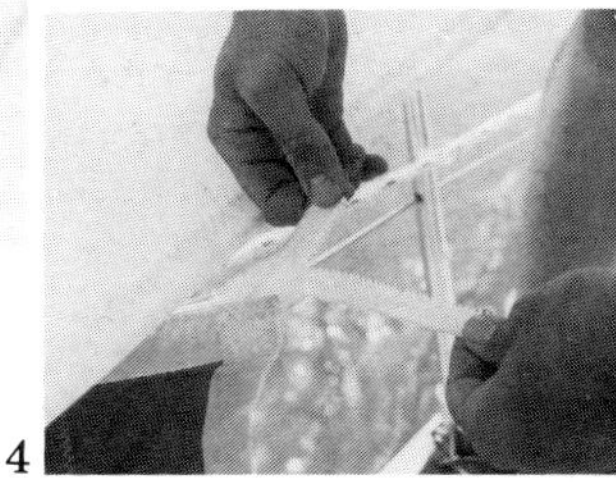

4

5

6

7

ABOVE *An outside hoist/inside drop. (1) The new sail goes into the headfoil outside the existing sail. (2) Pass the halyard forward, outside everything, and (3) clip on. (4) Open the bag of the new sail, (5) bend on the sheets, and (6) hoist the new sail. (7) Pull down the old sail. (8) If the old sail sticks, lift the skirt to allow air up between the two (the helmsman can help with a quick luff).*

8

ABOVE A tack change gives the best of both worlds: an inside hoist and an inside drop.

Tack change

The tack change alleviates the problem wholly. The yacht is tacked when the two sails are up and the old sail is fluttered down on deck as she comes through the eye of the wind. This is a fast and slick method, but requires good timing.

Things must be arranged so that the yacht is on the opposite tack to whichever halyard is set. Let us suppose she is on port tack with the set sail on the starboard halyard and in the starboard groove. (If it is in the port groove use a bare-headed change.) The new sail goes up inside the set sail on the port halyard and in the port groove. There is no need here to use a change sheet, for the lazy, weather sheet is unbent from the set sail and bent to the new sail from what is still the weather side. With the sail aloft, the yacht is tacked and the new sail sheeted home with the port-side sheet, the sheet of the old sail having been let go in the normal manner. As she comes through the eye of the wind the old halyard is let go and a quick tug on the luff brings the sail on deck with a will — and neatly inside the new sail. This method gives the best of both worlds: inside hoist and inside drop.

Final thoughts

With every sail change, remember to check that the sheet lead is right for the new sail, especially if the reason for the change is a turn in the course. The 'number three' does not usually set too well when sheeted to the same place as the blast reacher.

On three-halyard boats, the same principles apply, except that one is either going onto or coming off one of the spinnaker halyards. Times can arise when you are faced with the choice of doing a bare-headed change or intentionally crossing halyards. Suppose we are reaching on port with the number two genoa up on the genny halyard, port track, with the triradial on the starboard spinnaker halyard. The next leg

RIGHT "Sorry, Brian, we'll have to tack back." After changing sails or sheet leads, make sure everything is led correctly before you tack.

1

2

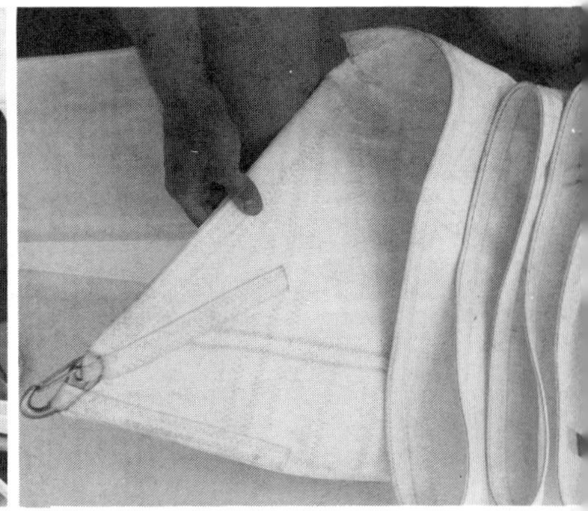

3

ABOVE *Never leave a sail unsecured on deck.*

is a beat, and we will want the number three genoa — it will either have to go up in the starboard groove but on the port spinnaker halyard, or the 'two' must be brought down and the 'three' sent up the starboard groove on the genny halyard.

On some boats the spinnaker halyards come out of the mast far enough above the headstay fitting for it to be safe to lead the halyard over the top — but now you must make sure that when the spinnaker comes down, it comes down to starboard of the mast and forestay. If the next mark is starboard-hand and the skipper for some reason decides to gybe the chute and then drop — the foredeck team are in big trouble. There has to be a very good reason for allowing halyards to cross intentionally. Most of us have enough trouble with the unintentional crosses we have to bear.

Once the old sail is down, the halyard is clipped either to the pulpit or back to the mast and the slack taken up straight away, before the loose, swinging halyard has a chance to hook round a spreader or to jump the sheave and jam at the masthead. Get the weight off the foredeck quickly by bringing the sail aft, along the weather deck if on the wind. Usually there will be time to bag the sail on deck before sending it below — stowed back in its proper place, not just dumped at the companion steps.

Often it may be felt that the change is only temporary and the sail just taken off may be the next one

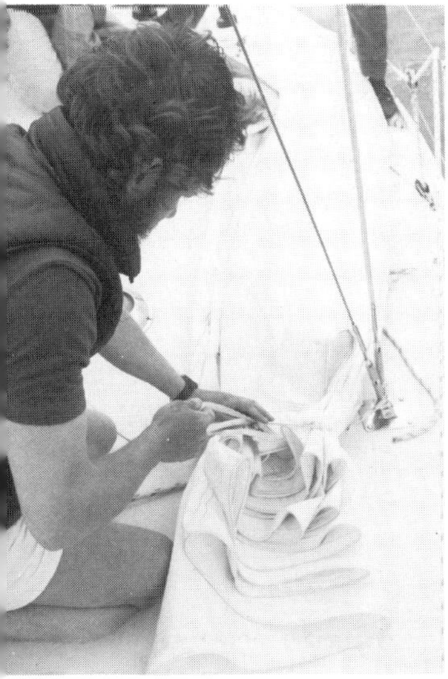

4

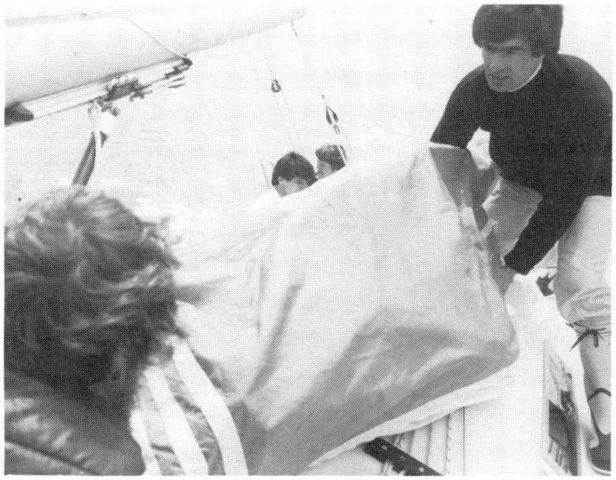

5

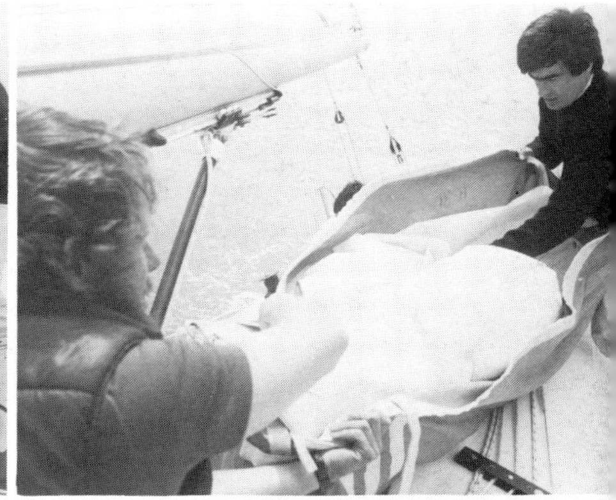

6

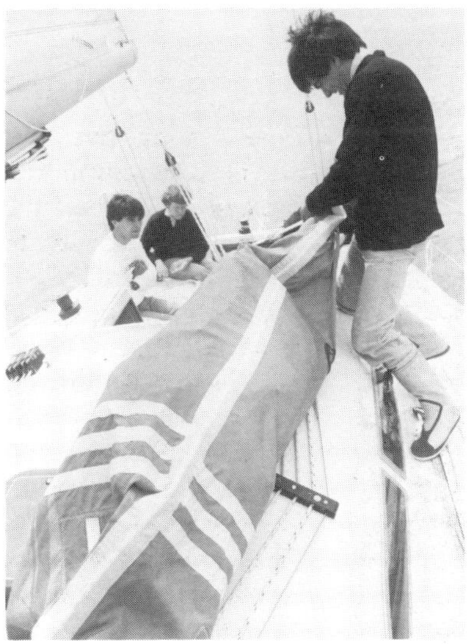

7

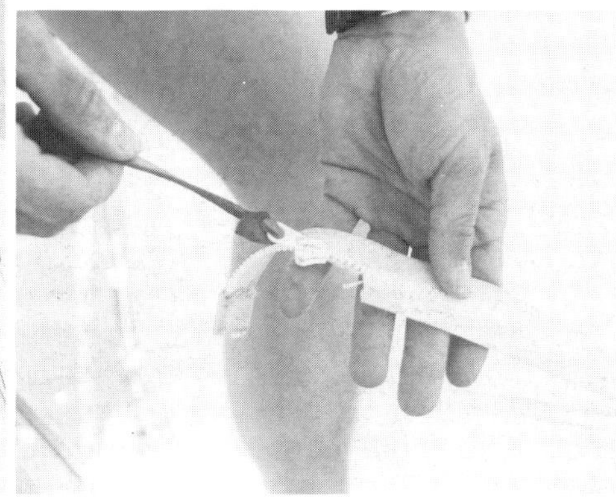

8

needed. Here the sail can be kept on deck, still tacked-down and lashed with sail-ties to the guard-rail or toe rail. Do not leave a sail thus all night, however, especially in conditions with spray on deck — bag it and send it below.

Finally, tidy up. Check the position of all the halyards, and their safe stowage. Check that the weather sheeting position has been altered to match the leeward one — and that the new weather sheet has been bent to the new sail. Check its lead (has the sheet crept under the spinnaker pole, or been passed inside the babystay?) so you are sure the yacht is clear to tack. "Just a minute" is not too helpful a reply to the order to tack with the yacht hurtling towards the shallows.

TOP *Bagging a sail on deck. In (5), (6) and (7) the bag is put over the sail upside down, the whole lot flipped the right way up and zipped. Note that the two tapes of the zipper should be staggered (8). The zip slide is pulled past the join and, when the time comes to open the bag, the two halves can be pulled apart without unzipping.*

4 · Trimming for windward speed

On a well-sailed dinghy the crew continually move their weight to compensate for gusts and lulls. Not only does this prevent the boat capsizing: she will sail faster and can be steered more easily if the crew react smartly to changes in the wind's strength.

The yacht sailing beside her has a ballast keel to prevent a capsize so the need to react to changes in the wind is less apparent. It is perfectly possible to trim her sails, cleat the sheets and sail to windward with only the helm being tended. The only problem is that if the yacht is sailed like this she will seldom win races; to do so her crew will need to trim the sails constantly and carefully — they are, after all, responding to the same changes in windspeed that keep the dinghy crew in continual motion.

On a yacht with a masthead rig the governing sail upwind is the genoa: it is much bigger than the mainsail and is working ahead of it, so it takes the wind first before passing it back to the mainsail. On a yacht with a fractional rig the main is more important although the headsail, being ahead, still has a profound effect on the trimming of the main.

On short inshore races it is relatively easy to give sail trim the attention it deserves: all the crew are on watch all the time, the best people stay on their allotted jobs all through the race, there are other yachts close by to outsail throughout the race, and it will not be uncommon for an inexperienced crew member to complete the race without touching the main or genoa sheets. But on a longer race constant attention to sail trim becomes the task of every crew member, for it is on a long race that the temptation simply to cleat the sheets and sail along is greatest: there may be no other yachts close by with which to compare speed, and what's a second or so in a day-and-a-half race? But look at it this way: in a 36-hour race with an average speed of 5 knots, an extra *hundreth* of a knot is worth over four minutes at the finish line. Even if we can't squeeze an extra 0.01 out of her, can we not make sure we don't drop a great deal more by failing to notice those slight changes in the breeze? Think of the dinghy sailor, constantly leaning out, leaning in, leaning out . . .

Trimming the genoa

The trimming tools available on the genoa are:

- the halyard
- the sheet
- The sheet lead position (both fore-and-aft and athwartships)
- the backstay (or runners, on boats that have them).

Coarse adjustment of the sheet is used to adjust the angle of the sail to the wind.,

Fine adjustment of the sheet and the halyard together are used to adjust the shape and fullness of the sail.

Movement of the sheet lead position is used to adjust the amount of twist in the sail.

Increasing backstay tension pulls the forestay tight (on a masthead rig) reducing luff sag.

All of these can be adjusted easily under load, except the sheet lead position. This is because the sheet pulls the slider upwards, making it impossible to move the lead block along the track. The trick is to pull that part of the sheet ahead of the block downwards, so the slider will move fore or aft along the track. On a smallish yacht this might be achieved just by pushing down on the sheet or by standing on it, perhaps easing the sheet slowly at the same time. On a bigger yacht more elaborate techniques are needed: if standing on the sheet does no more than improve the view you get of the other yachts, clip a

K 5
Humming Bird
R·T·Y·C

ABOVE *Use the spreaders as an aid to help you wind in the genoa sheet to the same extent each time.* OPPOSITE PAGE *Easing the genoa sheet a little adds fullness to the sail (left); easing it more alters the angle of the sail to the wind (right). Compare these sails with the fully sheeted genoa shown on the previous page.*

snatch block onto the sheet ahead of the lead block. Lead a line from it through a spare car further forward on the track (or through a spare lead block clipped to the toe rail) and then to a winch. Wind in on that line — easing the sheet at the same time — and the sheet will be pulled down to horizontal, allowing the lead block to be moved.

On some boats this system is permanently rigged in lieu of (or in conjunction with) conventional tracks and sliders.

How to trim the genoa

The main aids to trimming (apart from our own two eyes) are

- the telltales (every racing headsail should have three pairs positioned about 10 inches aft of the forestay at quarter, half and three-quarter height);
- the speedo;
- the panels of the sail itself (or better still, trim tapes — those thin black ribbons across the sail seen on the classier racers).

1· Set up the genoa by eye for today's conditions (the trim tapes will help here).
2· On a masthead yacht pull the backstay fairly tight. This in turn pulls the headfoil tight, taking much sag and round out of the luff of the genoa.
3· In smooth water and with a good breeze for the sail, trim for pointing ability. Reduce the fullness of the sail by tightening the halyard, but not so much that a crease appears in the form of a hard line down the luff. Tighten the sheet, but avoid pulling the sail taut around the base of the shrouds. The front part of the sail is now fairly flat, allowing the yacht to point high although she is critical to steer, there being only a narrow 'groove' in which she is going fast.
4· In a shifting breeze, or in waves where more power is needed (even at the expense of pointing) it may pay to ease halyard, sheet and backstay a little. This gives the genoa more round (the depth of the sail increases and the point of maximum draft moves forwards). The helmsman will find the boat less critical to steer on the wind, i.e. there is a broader 'groove'.

Using the telltales Next use the telltales to check you've got it right. Your objective is to provide the helmsman with three pairs of beautifully streaming telltales which all break together as the boat luffs. To get the telltales streaming ask the helmsman to hold the boat on the wind:

- If the windward telltales will not stream the sail is trimmed out too far. Check the helmsman isn't pinching, then wind in the sheet until the telltales stream.
- If the leeward telltales will not stream the sail is too close. Check the helmsman isn't off the wind, then ease the sheet until the telltales behave.

Next, ask the helmsman to luff slowly. All the windward or all the leeward telltales should move together.

- If the upper windward telltale misbehaves first, there is too much twist in the sail, cured either by tightening the halyard or moving the sheet lead forward.
- If the upper leeward telltale misbehaves but the lower telltales are streaming nicely, or if the lower windward telltale misbehaves while the upper telltales stream correctly, there is not enough twist to the sail and the halyard must be eased or the sheet lead moved aft.

A very easy way to discover what effect each con-

trol has on the sail is to overadjust each one in turn while leaving the others fixed (this is best tried when not racing). Set the sail up, then deliberately overtighten the halyard until the hard crease appears; now ease it and note what happens not just to the luff but also to the head of the sail — see how it starts tight and flat, the leech curling back inboard and perhaps against the upper spreader end, then how as the halyard is eased fullness appears in the head of the sail, the leech opens out until, with the halyard too soft, the leech at the head flutters, the luff becomes uncontrollable and the position of maximum draft moves aft until it is more than halfway between the luff and the leech.

Now do the same with the sheet lead, starting too far forward. See how the leech comes hard down from the headboard while the foot of the sail is so rounded and baggy it bellies out against the guardrail; move it aft and watch the leech open; see how twist grows in the sail until with the lead too far aft the leech flutters, the head of the sail will not fill and the foot is pulled flat and tight against the base of the shrouds. Watching the sail change shape will bring all the theory to life.

Trimming the main. THIS PAGE *Traveller up and mainsheet slack gives twist in the leech.* OPPOSITE *Traveller down and mainsheet tight closes the leech.*

Trimming the mainsail

The mainsail is controlled by:

- the halyard
- the outhaul
- the sheet
- the traveller
- the kicker (or vang)
- the cunningham
- the flattener
- the backstay and runners

The mainsail, with a rigid spar along two of its three sides, is easier to control than the genoa. On a fractional-rig yacht it is also more important than the genoa. Here again the trick of overtrimming each control in turn will illustrate dramatically the effect that each control has. Once again, we assume for simplicity that the boat has no runners.

1. The halyard and the outhaul adjust the shape and fullness of the sail.
2. The mainsheet is used on the wind principally to control the amount of twist in the mainsail.
3. The traveller controls the angle of the boom — and hence the sail — to the centreline of the yacht.

4· On the wind the kicker helps control the twist, and on yachts with powerful kickers and flexible booms it will be used to vary the depth of the sail at the bottom and near the mast.
5· The cunningham is merely an extension of the halyard's power. On virtually all yachts there is a maximum distance between the head of the mainsail and the bottom where the boom joins the mast (usually marked by black bands on light coloured masts, light bands on black masts) so the cunningham is needed to tighten the luff further when the sail is already at maximum height.
6· The backstay (on a fractional rig) controls mast bend and, therefore, fullness in the mainsail.

How to trim the mainsail

Sailing a fractional rigger upwind, the principal sail trimmer is most usually on the mainsail, using sheet and traveller in much the same way that the dinghy sailor's weight is used to keep the boat on her feet and moving freely.

Light and medium winds. The main aids to trimming are the telltales down the leech of the mainsail, ideally positioned one at each batten pocket. Your objective is to keep all the telltales streaming and have very little backwinding in the front of the main.

Firstly use the traveller and mainsheet to align the main boom down the centreline of the boat.

- If all the telltales are streaming gradually increase mainsheet tension, at the same time letting the traveller down to leeward so the boom stays on the centreline. You are reducing twist in the sail — continue to do this until the top telltale begins to curl in behind the sail.
- If the top telltale(s) are misbehaving let off the mainsheet, at the same time pulling the traveller up to windward. The boom stays on the centreline and the sail twists until the telltales stream again.

Stronger winds. While the mainsheet controls mainsail shape, the traveller controls its angle of attack and is to the fractional-rig yacht what the accelerator pedal is to a motor car. If the yacht seems overpowered, ease the traveller down, if she is underpowered (most likely with dead or with lee helm), bring the traveller up until full power is restored. In gusty conditions the traveller will have to be dumped frequently, but if it spends more time dumped than putting on power, it is time to reef.

The main traveller has a profound effect on something other than just the mainsail: the rudder. As the power comes on and off the mainsail, the effect on feel and rudder balance is enormous. Here, the helmsman and trimmer must communicate continuously: on the best boats they use few words, for the trimmer can tell just by watching the wheel or tiller how much helm the yacht is needing, and apply power or ease it as required.

Runners. Runners are adjustable lines that run from the middle section of the mast down to the side deck near the stern. There may be one or more runners on each side of the boat.

On a masthead-rig boat the runners simply control mast bend: increasing runner tension reduces mast bend and so increases the fullness in the mainsail. On a fractional rig the upper runners meet the mast near the hounds, so increasing runner tension tightens the headstay. If a set of lower runners (checkstays) are fitted they are used to control mast bend.

Reefing

All the crew become involved when it is time for the flattener or for a reef to go in. Slab reefing is now virtually universal, and systems are almost standard. The depth of the reef is dictated by the position of the reef cringles at luff and leech. Usually the luff cringle is fitted over a hook at the gooseneck, and the leech cringle pulled down by a line made fast at the boom end, rove through the cringle, down into or along the boom and brought out at the mast. It is then led down the mast and back to a winch.

Reefing procedure is simple, but if each step is not taken logically much sweat and even breakage can result. We need to tend the halyard, the reefing line, the kicker, the mainsheet and the luff of the main-

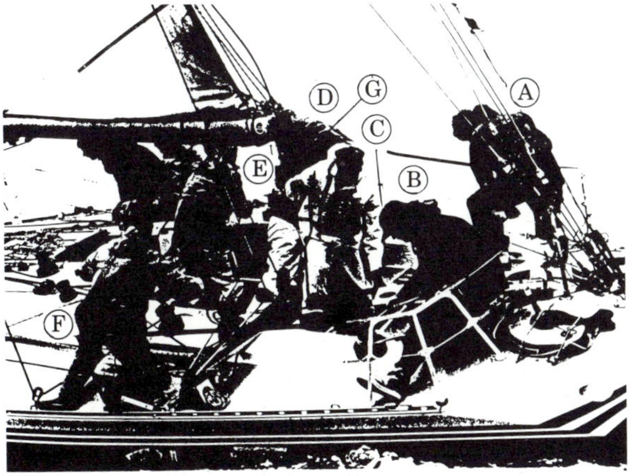

Basic tacking skills: the crew of the British Admiral's Cup yacht 'Black Topic' shows how it should be done. The helmsman (C) has put the helm down and moves across the boat. Even as she begins to turn, crewman (A) has the old runner tail in hand ready to let it off; (B) hauls in the slack on the new runner, which he will make up hard as the yacht comes up head-to-wind. Behind the helmsman the main trimmer (G) prepares to move the mainsheet car across the track. As the weight comes out of the genoa the port trimmer (F) throws the old genoa sheet off its winch while tailer (E) starts to haul in the new sheet. The starboard trimmer (D) is ready with the winch handle as the spare crew start to move across the boat. The bowman has already moved up into the pulpit to haul in some of the genoa foot as the boat comes through the wind's eye, thus helping the clew of the sail round the mast, saving wear and smoothing the tack; once the clew is past the mast he will let the sail go to be sheeted home.

sail. Never begin reefing until each member of the team knows which controls he or she will attend. When all is ready:

1· Ease the halyard (the immediate effect will be that the boom will drop markedly, which is probably why so many crews neglect to ease the sheet and kicker later).
2· Pull the luff down, fit the ring over the hook and take up on the halyard straight away, to prevent the ring from falling off the hook again.
3· *Ease both the sheet and the kicker*. Then take up the slack on the reefing line, take turns on the winch and wind in the reef.

Note that it is imperative to ease both sheet and kicker, otherwise the winch winder has to wind against these, effectively trimming the sail by the reefline alone. It is likely that the reef cringle will be pulled out of the leech of the sail, or the reefing line will break under the enormous load, or the mainsheet or kicker fittings will start to pull out of the boom.

Some crews are reluctant to ease that mainsheet right away, thinking that by keeping some power in the mainsail through the reefing process they are losing less speed. The opposite is usually the truth: the sheet is eased right away, the sail flogs briefly, the reefing line is banged home and the sail re-trimmed within a few seconds.

In, out, on and off

Finally, a word about communication. While you're trimming you may find the helmsman using a cryptic code which the newcomer finds either confusing or just unintelligible. Most controls move up or down, in or out, or backwards or forwards. Many instructions call merely for 'on' and 'off': but the logic is very simple. Whatever movement of the control gives the yacht more power is 'on', and the opposite is 'off'. Thus 'sheet on' is sheet in; 'runner off' is runner tail eased, and so on.

Some calls require more than one control to be moved. 'Main off' usually means traveller down, but also require the sheet to be eased as well; 'main on' will usually mean traveller up (pulling the boom in) and mainsheet in (pulling the boom down).

1

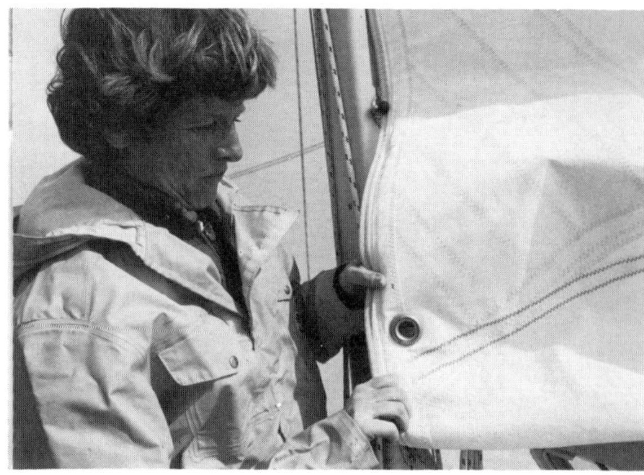

4

Reefing the main. Reeve and tie off the reefing pennant (1, 2, 3). Ease the halyard, hook in the reef tack cringle and retension the halyard (4, 5). Ease the kicker and sheet (6, 7) and wind in the reefing pennant. Finally retension the sheet and kicker.

2

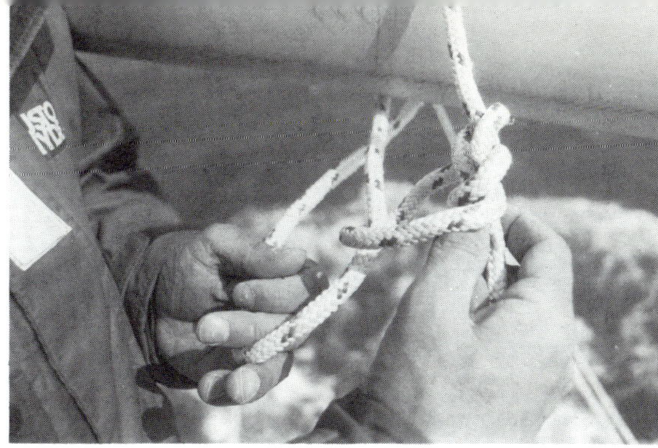

3

5

6

7

8

5 · White-sail reaching

Yachts which go distance and passage racing, indeed any that race off an Olympic triangle, spend much time with the sheets just eased: not hard on the wind, but at the same time not far enough off to carry a spinnaker. This facet of racing is pure boatspeed and little else; but it can call for a fair amount of sail handling and plenty of crew work — much more than sailing hard on the wind.

In smooth water the helmsman should be steering as straight as a die while the trimmers adjust the sails not merely to the changes in wind strength but also to the wind direction, using the speedometer as the final adjudicator of their success. Just how straight a course is steered depends on how good the helmsman is and on the rapport between helmsman and trimmers: the hallowed dinghy technique of 'up in the lulls' and 'away in the puffs' does not work so well, if at all, on bigger yachts which do not plane.

We call this white-sail reaching because only the fore-and-aft sails are used: on yachts up to 33 ft these will usually be simply the mainsail and number one genoa (probably the light number one if there is a choice, as it will usually have a higher clew and be fuller cut than the heavy); on bigger yachts there will probably be a specialised reaching jib, and perhaps a staysail to set inside the reacher.

Trimming the genoa

As the wind hauls aft and the sheets are eased we trim for speed, and the first rule of thumb is trim the genoa, *then* the mainsail. In white-sail reaching the slot between genoa and mainsail is every bit as important as in upwind sailing.

As the genoa sheet is eased the clew of the sail will rise, throwing more twist into the sail. More twist will be required anyway, to keep the slot open at the top once the mainsail is eased, but if there is too much twist the top of the sail will not fill and drive when the bottom is right: and if the top is set right, the lower part of the sail will be overtrimmed, backwinding the main.

Here again the telltales are valuable. The genoa will work within a wider range of angles of attack than when on the wind, and it will be possible to ease the sheet and have the weather telltale lifting long before there is any suggestion of the luff backfilling. The rule of thumb here is to trim to the leeward telltale, and often the windward telltale will be lifting considerably.

As the wind hauls further aft — say to about 50 degrees apparent — the weather telltale can be ignored completely, for it will be hanging lifeless inside the sail where it curves away from the forestay. As long as the three leeward telltales are working together, the twist is about right. The leech of the genoa and the leech of the main should follow similar curves till they meet at the masthead, while on a fractional rig, the leech of the genoa should be following the curve of the mainsail's belly.

As twist increases, the top of the sail will stop working — the misbehaving telltale being the first sign. Now is the time to start moving the sheet lead position forward, to take out some of the twist. Unfortunately, moving the lead forward also tends to pull the clew of the sail inboard, just when we want it outboard (to open the slot and to leave room for the mainsail to be eased as well).

Barber-hauling the genoa. The lead is moved outboard progressively, moving the clew of the sail and opening the slot while controlling twist. Compare the shape of the genoa shown opposite (barber-hauler off) with that shown on page 43 (barber-hauler on).

Humming Bird
R·T·Y·C

So we need a way of moving the lead position not merely forward but outboard and downwards as well. For this we use a barber-hauler: a snatch block clipped onto the sheet between the lead block and the clew. A line from the snatch block is led through another block clipped to the toe rail to a winch, and this is winched-in as the sheet is eased. The effect is to pull the sheet out of line and, provided the toe-rail block is correctly positioned, we can adjust the sheet and the barber-hauler until we have the clew of the sail just where we want it.

Trimming the mainsail

With the genoa trimmed we turn our attention to the mainsail. Yet again, the telltales — this time off the leech of the sail — are our principal guide to how well the sail is working, whilst the tools at our disposal are the sheet, the traveller, the kicker, the halyard and the outhaul.

If the true wind strength remains constant the apparent wind speed — the speed across the deck it is sometimes called — will drop as the yacht bears away onto a close reach. This, combined with the change of angle, will require all the mainsail controls to be reset. The halyard and the outhaul must be eased, the traveller let down to put the boom at the desired angle and the sheet eased to put more twist into the sail. The kicker will probably need to be eased too.

Crew weight will have to be kept aft, more so than when beating, and on very wide-stern boats with the maximum beam far aft, it may already be time for one or two crew members to move their weight aft of the helmsman. You get a great view, perched on the aft pulpit.

Other reaching sails

By now it may be time for the *high-clew reacher*, if the sail inventory includes one. This is set exactly like an ordinary headsail, using a full-height halyard and the luff groove on the headstay. Because of the high clew the sheet lead position will be well aft, but because the sail is specially designed for this point of sailing it will seldom be necessary to barber-haul it.

Staysails are seldom worth the effort on yachts under 30 ft, because what they add to the speed is often more than subtracted by the speed loss incurred through the disturbance of setting and trimming them; but on bigger yachts they are used a good deal.

'Staysail' is a complete misnomer — yet one more example of modern yacht usage taking an age-old seaman's word and turning it upside down — because the sail is not set on a stay at all but is set flying, inside the curve of the reacher. Whereas the reacher is cut with a high clew, the staysail is cut with a very low clew and its job is to increase the flow of air through the slot between the reacher and the mainsail — in particular low down where air is 'escaping' under the high-cut foot of the reacher.

The yacht may have a staysail purely for use with the reacher, or she may have a dual-purpose sail for this job and as spinnaker staysail. The reaching staysail has a shorter luff and foot: the dual-purpose staysail will have a full-height luff but with extra cringles part of the way up the luff to act as the tack when reaching and at the leech to act as the clew.

The reaching staysail is tacked down to a deck fitting not quite halfway aft between the forestay and the mast: often the tack fitting is on a track, to allow adjustment. A single sheet is all that is required, led to a fairlead forward of and inboard of the reacher sheet lead. If there is a staysail halyard, it will emerge from the mast at about two-thirds height, otherwise a spare masthead halyard is used. Fractional-rig yachts seldom use staysails — there is just not enough room in the foretriangle.

LEFT Using a snatch block to barber-haul on a big yacht.
OPPOSITE The effect of barber-hauling (compare with page 41).

Humming Bird
R·T·Y·C

6 · Setting the spinnaker

No sail provides a greater single test of a yacht's crew than the spinnaker. By watching how the spinnaker is set, trimmed, gybed and handed ('dropped' is a word we might care to avoid — too often it is only too accurate a description of what has happened), observers can most easily pick out the well-crewed yacht from the badly crewed yacht, and badly crewed yachts have to have big reserves of boatspeed or very good navigators if they are to win races regularly. By the same token, the crew member who can approach Spinnaker Time with confidence and competence is worth half-a-dozen tactical experts as the gybe mark looms ahead.

Yet spinnaker work is like most other crewing tasks: it just needs common sense and logic. Its special ingredient, however, is team work. Only on the smallest boats can the spinnaker be handled completely by one person: on a Quarter Tonner the team will usually be two, one doing the deck work and the halyard, one tending the lines (topping lift and downhaul, sheet and guy) in the cockpit. On a 30-footer there might be four: one on the foredeck, one at the mast and two in the cockpit. Each member of the team must have his or her assigned tasks and responsibilities: unless the team has worked together often and recently, talk each manoeuvre — hoisting, gybing or whatever — through beforehand to make sure everyone is expecting the same thing to happen in the same order. One person doing the wrong thing at the wrong time can wreck an otherwise beautiful day.

Spinnaker gear

Halyards. All but the simplest one-designs will have two spinnaker halyards, usually of flexible wire with rope tails. The spinnaker halyards always emerge from the mast above the point where the forestay joins the mast (even on a masthead-rigged boat) so that the spinnaker, when set, is free to swing across the front of the forestay, setting on the port or starboard side of the yacht as required, or being shifted across when gybing.

Unlike the mainsail or genoa halyard, the spinnaker halyard is not played as part of the sail controls: the spinnaker is either up, or it is not up. In all but the smallest boats, however, the halyard will nonetheless be taken to a winch. This is primarily to give control over the halyard when the time comes to lower the sail: in hoisting the spinnaker, the sail should be virtually at the masthead before there is any real weight on the halyard, other than the weight of the cloth, and good crews on even quite big boats can have the sail aloft by hand using the winch only for the final few feet of halyard.

Topping lift and downhaul. The topping lift and the downhaul (on bigger boats called the foreguy) will also be led to winches. Even on a 22 ft masthead-rig yacht, the spinnaker is big enough to pull against a strong man unless the mechanical advantage of a winch is used.

Pole systems

The spinnaker pole is the all-important element in controlling the spinnaker. The sail itself is probably the biggest sail on the boat, yet it is set in certainly the most precarious manner. Therefore the pole must act as a rigid spar to hold the outer corner of the spinnaker, and to do this it must itself be rigid, and held firmly in place.

This is achieved by having the inboard end of the pole secured to the mast, the outboard end held firm by the triangulated support given by the topping lift (holding it up), the foreguy (holding it downwards

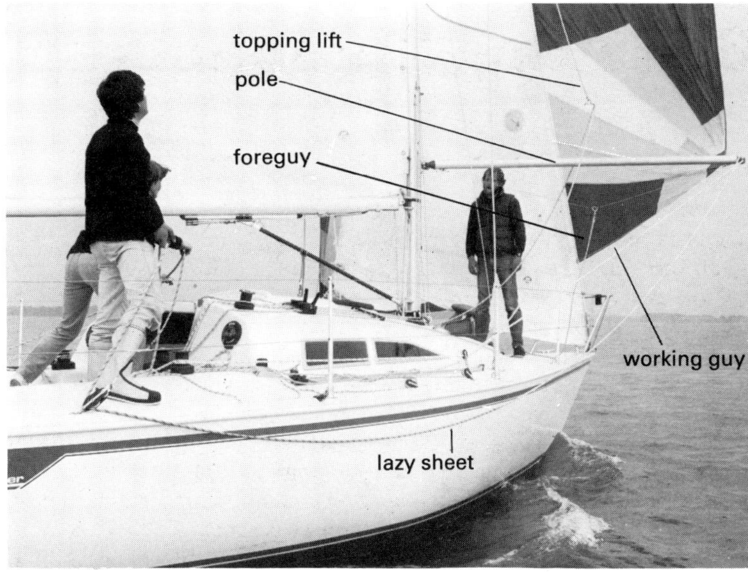

RIGHT *Spinnaker gear*

and forwards) and the spinnaker guy itself, pulling it downwards and aft.

The bigger the boat and the bigger the spinnaker, the bigger, stronger and more complex must be the pole and its rigging. On the largest yachts it may take three men to lift the pole, lock it onto its mast fitting and winch it aloft with the topping lift acting like the jib of a crane.

Double-ended pole. This is the simplest system, like that used in most dinghies except that in yachts the pole is not stowed along the main boom but on the foredeck. The pole itself is light enough to be handled by one person and has identical fittings at either end. One end clips to the mast fitting, the guy runs through the other. *Note that the spinnaker pole should never be attached directly to the sail.*

To gybe the double-ended pole, the inboard end is unclipped from the mast, passed across the foredeck to the sheet and clipped to that. The outboard end is unclipped from the guy, the pole is pushed right across and what was the outboard end now becomes the inboard end and is clipped to the mast. Through all this, the pole is supported by the topping lift, and to keep the pole balanced this support must be spread evenly along the length of the pole. This is achieved by having the topping lift come to the middle of a wire span or bridle which itself is secured to the two ends of the pole. The downhaul goes to the middle of a similar bridle, underneath the pole. (Topping lift and downhaul are not attached directly to the middle of the pole because the spinnaker itself acts on the end of the pole, and to attach the pole supports to the middle would cause it to bend and probably break).

With this system, only one line is needed to each corner of the spinnaker, acting as both sheet and guy. The lead from the deck will be varied, using a snatch block or a simple barber-hauler, depending on whether the line is acting as sheet or guy.

This system is usually found on masthead-rig boats up to about 27 ft, but can be used on fractional-rig boats up to about 33 ft: it all depends on the size of the spinnaker.

Single-ended pole. When the size of the spinnaker requires a pole too heavy to be swung about the

ABOVE *From left — lazy guy, sheet, jibsheet over pole, guy, lazy sheet.*

foredeck by one person, or when the sail is too big to be gybed dinghy-style, the safer but slower single-ended pole is used.

The fittings are usually different at either end, with a plunger or latch-operated clip at the outboard end through which runs the guy, and a conical plug at the inboard end which fits into a cup on the mast. The cup on the mast is mounted on a slider which runs on a track on the fore side of the mast, allowing the height of the pole to be adjusted.

The type of pole fitted and the gybing technique used go hand in hand. With a single-ended pole, the so-called dip-pole gybe is used (see chapter 8).

For dip-pole gybing it is necessary to have two lines to each corner of the spinnaker, not one. We have a separate guy and sheet rigged on each side, and the line not in use is called the *lazy guy* or *lazy sheet.* For example, on port gybe, the pole will be on the port side and the sail trimmed with the port-side guy and the starboard-side sheet; the port-side sheet, although attached to the sail, is doing no work and is called the lazy sheet; the starboard-side guy is also doing no work, and is thus the lazy guy. On the other gybe, the port-side guy is the lazy guy, the starboard-side sheet the lazy sheet.

Having gone to the expense of duplicating the sheet and guy on each side, we can take advantage of their presence to refine the system. Usually, sheet and guy will be led differently (the guy being led further forward than the sheet), and different types of rope can be used for each. The guy takes greater loads than the sheet and must not stretch, whereas a bit of stretch in the sheet is no bad thing. The guy will usually thus be heavier than the sheet, and may be of a low-stretch rope such as Kevlar-core. It is always the sheet which is attached to the sail, the guy being attached to the end-fitting of the sheet, usually by a clip onto a stainless steel ring. This is to facilitate letting go the tack of the spinnaker when the time comes to hand the sail (see chapter 10).

With a single-ended pole, the topping lift and downhaul (on bigger yachts usually called the foreguy, because it is led in a different way to the smaller yacht's downhaul) can be taken direct to the outboard end of

TOP, LEFT *Single-ended pole arrangement.* CENTRE *Correctly rigged — sheet over guy.* TOP RIGHT *Incorrectly rigged — the lazy sheet under the pole results in problems when gybing* (RIGHT).

the pole. Indeed, the foreguy is normally left clipped on, and is used to secure the pole in the stowed position.

Dual system. Masthead-rig yachts of around 30 ft to 32 ft often combine these two systems, using a double-ended pole with duplicated lines. This allows flexibility in crewing since the style of gybe (end-for-end or dip-pole) can be selected depending on the weather conditions.

Twin poles. This system is rarely met with now, but is basically two single-ended poles, one port and one starboard. The two poles are only used together when gybing, the leeward pole being set up before the gybe, the sail being gybed onto it and the old pole, now the leeward pole, being taken away.

Hoisting the spinnaker

Remember the 'five peas': Proper Preparation Prevents Poor Performance. Make everything ready before the spinnaker is needed, then as little time as possible need be spent on the foredeck before the spinnaker is ready for hoisting.

To button-on the the spinnaker, we need:

- the sail on deck, and the sail bag or turtle attached to something so that it will not blow overboard;
- the sheet and guys led correctly to the correct corners of the spinnaker, and attached;
- the halyard attached to the head (not the clew) of the spinnaker;
- the pole clipped to the mast and set up on the topping lift with the guy led through the outboard end of the pole.

The Golden Rule is **everything must be led outside everything else**.

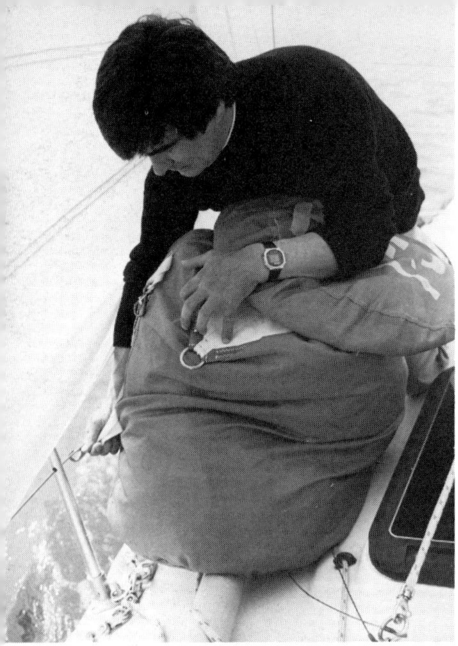

1

2

3

The sail in the bag. The bag or turtle with the sail properly packed inside (see chapter 10) must be brought on deck to the place where the sail will be launched. On small boats this will be the pulpit; on bigger boats the lee rail, under and outboard of the genoa. Use the tie-tapes on the underside of the turtle to tie it to something solid to prevent it blowing overboard when the sail is hauled out. Spinnaker turtles are not merely expensive, they are difficult to make during a race and you may need it again before the finish.

Sheets and guys. Lead the sheets and guys to the turtle. The windward pair, which will be the guy and lazy sheet, must go outboard of the windward shrouds, outboard and forward of the forestay and to the sail, coming over the top of the guardrail. The sheet and lazy guy come round the leeward rigging and over the top of the guardrail. Although the spinnaker will set as well inside-out as outside-out, most will have a green patch at one lower corner and a red patch at the other. The sail should have been packed with the green (starboard) patch to the right of the head and the red (port) patch to the left, so it makes good sense to follow the convention and position the turtle with the corners pointing the right way (green to what will be the starboard side when the sail is up, red to what will be the port side) and then clip the starboard lines to the green corner and the port lines to the red corner. All this lessens the chance of the sail going up with a twist in it.

Halyard. It also means that the only corner left unattached and to which the halyard can be clipped is the head, which is usually white. It is very embarrassing to hoist a spinnaker on its side with the halyard clipped to the clew, but some of the best crews in the world have done it — which shows that it is also very easy. If there is a choice, use the leeward spinnaker halyard, leading it outside the genoa and over the top guardrail to the sail. If the windward halyard must be used (after several sail changes, it may be that the headsail is on the leeward spinnaker halyard) make sure that it leads clear from the masthead *over* the forestay and down to the sail. Remember: everything outside everything else.

Setting the pole

Note that the pole is used with the end clips opening *upwards*. Unship the pole from its stowage, make

5

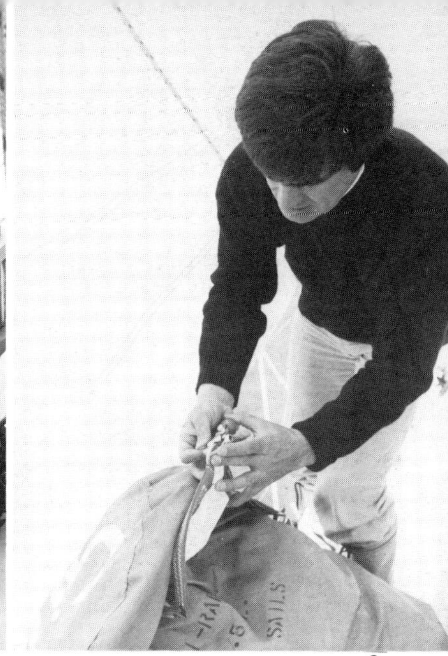

6

ABOVE Hoisting the spinnaker. Secure the bag (1) and clip on the sheets (2). Set the pole (3) and lead the guy (4). Clip on the halyard (5, 6); all set to wind in the halyard and guy (right).

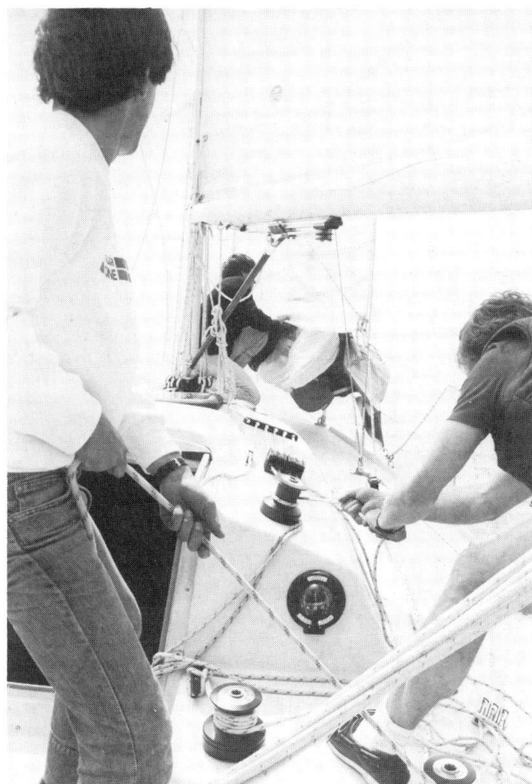

sure that the downhaul (or foreguy) and the topping lift are tended and free to run. Clip on both. Put the inboard end to the mast fitting, with the outboard end lying on deck where it is free to lift without catching under the guardrails or pulpit, or under the genoa. The best place is lying to weather of the forestay, inside the pulpit legs.

The foredeck hand supports the outboard end of the pole while the weight is taken on the topping lift, partly raising the pole until it rests against the weather side of the forestay. Pause here to put the guy through the end fitting of the pole, *making sure that the lazy sheet lies on top of the pole.* This is very important. If the lazy sheet hangs under the pole when the time comes to gybe, the pole cannot drop down free from the guy but becomes caught between the guy and lazy sheet. This spells trouble in a big way, the most expensive version being where the pole ends up sticking out through the front of the spinnaker.

Top up the pole to the required height, and the foredeck department is ready to go.

Meanwhile, Back Aft

In the cockpit, things must be happening to support what is going on at the front of the boat. The sheet and guys must be tended, principally to see that the foredeck hand has enough slack, but also to see that there is not too much slack, with lines going over the side, round the rudder, propeller or even the keel. The topping lift and foreguy must be tended constantly, and when the pole is being set it is important to ensure that there is plenty of slack in the weather guy and sheet. If there is not, the corner of the sail will be pulled out of the turtle as pole is raised, will fill with wind and pull the rest of the sail out. This will happen behind the genoa and probably not be seen until the sail appears in a bundle in the water alongside the cockpit. Everybody will notice then.

Here we go

Everything is ready. Make sure that there is:

- someone on the halyard, with back-up if needed;
- someone on the sheet;
- someone on the guy;
- they all know what is going to happen when the cat comes out of the bag, and what they have to do.

If necessary, the crew leader should talk through the operation with everyone, so that all know exactly what is happening, what they have to do and that nothing has been forgotten.

The order to hoist should be given either by the skipper if on deck, or by the watch leader. Everyone must know beforehand whose voice will give the signal, and that person must be very sure that the yacht is ready for her spinnaker. Do not forget to check with the helmsman — many is the spinnaker that has started its way aloft while the helmsman was still trying to shave past the mark. If the sail touches the

mark the yacht may be disqualified, and all that slickness and preparation have been for naught.

Hit it!

The spinnaker in the bag is safe and easily controlled. The spinnaker filled with wind but firmly held at head, clew and tack is safe and easily controlled. Between these two states, the spinnaker is just trouble looking for somewhere to happen — so it stands to reason that the shorter can be kept the transitional stage, the better. The Golden Rule is **get it up, then get it in**.

The head of the sail should come out of the bag first, followed by the tack. As the head rockets toward the mast the tack should be springing toward the pole end: the clew can look after itself.

Thus as the halyard is taken up, the guy should also be taken in, fast, to pull the tack back to the pole. Do not wait until the sail is up before hauling aft the guy.

If the sail is launched in this manner, the clew will blow away to leeward as the tack (and with it the luff of the spinnaker) comes round the forestay and finds the wind. Then, when the sail is properly up and the halyard secure, the sheet can be taken in and trimmed and the sail will fill beautifully. If, however, the sheet is trimmed too soon, the spinnaker is pulled into the windshadow of the genoa and mainsail where there is no wind to fill it. As the guy is, belatedly, hauled aft the clew drags across the back of the genoa, the foot tightens across the back of the genoa and soon the genoa stops working as well. The boat slows right down, just when she should be accelerating. So:

- halyard first and fast;
- guy next and quickly;
- sheet in when it's up.

BELOW *Hoisting the spinnaker. The halyard and guy should be wound in almost together, then the sheet pulled in as the spinnaker goes up.*

ABOVE *Undoing a twist. Pull on the luff; if that doesn't work, ease the halyard as well.*

Don't overwork the halyard grinder. The other problem with sheeting in too quickly is that the sail fills before the halyard is right up and secured. At best this means that the last few feet of halyard have to be ground in, which is just unnecessary hard work; at worst, the weight in the sail defeats the halyard grinder, the halyard runs back out and the sail falls in the water.

The gybe set

We have described the conventional leeward set, with plenty of time to make ready and set the pole. Sometimes the race dictates we approach a windward mark on one tack, round it, gybe and go away on the opposite gybe. During this manoeuvre, the spinnaker has somehow to appear.

Everything is made ready as before, except with the spinnaker on what is still the windward side. However, we cannot set the pole up, because the genoa is in the way: but we can be very nearly ready.

Setting the pole. Clip the pole to the mast in the normal manner, but with the outboard end out under the genoa, using the foreguy to keep the pole end close to the forestay. The pole end must not drag in the water, or be allowed to slide down and out under the leeward guardrail. The topping lift is clipped on but left slack, making sure that it has been led *under the genoa sheet.*

As the yacht bears away into the gybe, the genoa is eased out and quickly pulled across the pole. As soon as the genoa is across, the pole can be topped up in the normal way and the spinnaker set.

7 · Trimming the spinnaker

A spinnaker is just a spinnaker, no matter how big the boat, so the rules for trimming it on a yacht are the same as on a dinghy. The difference lies in the size of the sail and the power it produces: the spinnaker on even a small masthead-rig yacht will produce more than enough power to pull a crewman off his feet and over the side. So the mechanics of big-boat spinnakers are more complex.

Turns on the winch

Both the sheet and the guy must be led to winches and the first Golden Rule of spinnaker trimming is **never take it off the winch**. The guy should always have at least two turns round the winch; while for the sheet, the number of turns will be whatever is needed to grip the sheet so that there is no pull on the trimmer's arm with the sail full and drawing. In very light weather there might be just one turn on the winch so that the sail can be given sheet each time it needs it, and in a breeze three turns may be needed.

In ghosting conditions even one full turn may be too much on a small spinnaker; the sail will not draw the sheet out against even that small amount of friction. In such conditions (by which time lightweight light-weather sheets will have been rigged) take the turn off the winch but continue to lead the sheet from the turning block round the winch barrel to your hand. This way (apart from giving the correct lead) you still have the friction of a half-a-turn round the barrel of the winch to help cope with stray gusts and cat's-paws, and if the wind does pick up quickly a complete turn can be put on in a twinkling. Taking the sheet right off the winch, to lead straight to hand from the turning block, sooner or later results in rope-burned palms. Don't do it.

On yachts over 30 ft, even the topping lift and downhaul must be worked on winches all the time.

Organisation

It is the size of the spinnaker, rather than the size of the yacht, which determines spinnaker organisation, but as a guide we can equate a 27 ft masthead-rig yacht with a 33 ft fractional. Above this size, trimming the spinnaker sheet is a two-person job. The trimmer has to hand the tail of the sheet, and stands or sits wherever he or she has the best view of the sail (some of the best spinnaker trimmers on smaller yachts — where brute strength is not needed — are women). The winder is positioned at the winch, with the task of cranking the winch every time the trimmer calls the sheet in. With enough weight in the sail for this to be required, a minimum of two turns will be needed just to stop the winch barrel slipping inside

BELOW Winching for the tailer.

the turns of the sheet, but with more than three turns it will be difficult to get the sheet to run out sweetly to ease the sail.

Basic trimming rules

- The spinnaker should be symmetrical about its own vertical midline.
- Unless the boat is being overpowered the spinnaker should be shaped and trimmed to present the maximum possible area (called the projected area) to the wind.
- The spinnaker pole should be at right angles to the direction of the apparent wind (the wind across the deck).
- The tack and the clew of the sail must be at the same height off the deck; thus the foot of the sail is horizontal.
- The pole should be horizontal, or slightly cocked upwards at the outboard end. The pole should never point downwards from the mast.

ABOVE *Pole too low — clews not level, luff too tight, sail twisted to windward.*

The pole

Once the sail is up and drawing, the helmsman should steady the boat on the required course. With the boat on course, bring the pole aft (by winding in on the guy) until the luff of the spinnaker starts to collapse by folding in on itself. The guy should then be eased out, allowing the pole to go forward, by three or four inches — just enough to stop the luff curling.

Remember that every time the guy is moved the foreguy (or downhaul) which is acting against it, must be tended also.

The sheet

With the pole and guy properly set, ease the sheet until once again the luff of the sail starts to fold in upon itself, then pull the sheet in about four inches, until the luff stops folding. The sheet and guy are now correctly set.

Because the direction of the wind is never constant, the spinnaker sheet must be constantly on the move. Even if the true wind remained constant in direction and speed, the very act of trimming the spinnaker correctly affects boatspeed and thus apparent wind. Trim the spinnaker properly and the yacht immediately picks up speed. As she accelerates the apparent wind draws slightly ahead, requiring the sheet to be brought in. The boat reaches her maximum speed for that breeze and is no longer accelerating: the apparent wind draws aft again and the spinnaker is now overtrimmed. The boat starts to slow. All these minor changes in apparent wind direction can be dealt with by the spinnaker sheet, but it must constantly be on the move. The Golden Rule of spinnaker trimming is **ease it**. For every properly trimmed spinnaker in the fleet, there are two which are oversheeted.

Pole height

Outboard end. The clew of the sail, to which the sheet is attached, is free to find its own height naturally, depending on the trim of the spinnaker, the shape of the sail and the amount of wind. The tack, attached to the pole, should be kept at the same height and to do this the outboard end of the pole must be

Pole too high — sail twisted to leeward.

About right, but the inboard end of the pole should be raised.

moved up or down as appropriate. With a good breeze, the wind in the sail will tend to lift the pole, so to raise the pole it is necessary only to ease the foreguy and the outboard end will rise.

If there is little wind, the pole's own weight will be pulling it and the spinnaker downwards, and the pole end must then be adjusted on the topping lift, remembering first to slacken the foreguy to allow the pole end to lift.

To lower the tack, first ease the topping lift. If the pole does not drop by its own weight, it will have to be winched down with the downhaul or foreguy.

Inboard end. With the outboard end set, the inboard end must be moved to keep the pole horizontal: this keeps the outboard end of the spinnaker as far away from the mast as possible, thus giving the maximum projected area of sail. Ideally the pole should be horizontal or slightly cocked upwards. If the pole is allowed to get too far out of horizontal, especially if the outboard end is below the level of the inboard end, there is a danger of the inward thrusting forces on the end of the pole causing it to capsize, the inboard end scooting up to the stopper on the top end of the mast track and the outer end slamming down onto the deck. Naturally, this does not apply to small yachts with only a fixed ring attachment at the mast for the pole.

Keep it rigid. Remember every time the pole height is adjusted that the foreguy and the topping lift must be tightened up to keep the pole end rigid under the tack of the spinnaker. If the pole end is allowed to slop about, all it does is shake the air out of the spinnaker. Conversely, remember always to ease the foreguy before trying to move the inboard end of the pole. This will reduce the inward-thrusting forces and take the weight off the pole and the slider on the mast track.

Rules for running

Straight downwind, or very broad reaching, the yacht stays more or less upright and the spinnaker is at its best, virtually all its power being used to pull the yacht along, little being used in heeling her over or dragging her sideways.

Weight aft

Because it is attached near the top of the mast, the spinnaker pulling forward on the yacht well above the waterline exerts a turning force which acts to push the bows down into the water. For this reason, the harder it blows the more weight there has to be aft to help lift the bows; running fast downwind in a blow, virtually all the crew move aft, sometimes aft of the helmsman.

Preventing rolling

Rolling is the biggest problem when sailing straight downwind under spinnaker, particularly in heavy airs and big seas when things can become so bad that the boat becomes unmanageable. As well as the obvious effects of hurling everyone off their feet and smashing the crockery down below, heavy rolling makes the boat very difficult to steer because of the rapid and dramatic changes to the immersed shape.

The rolling is caused largely by the spinnaker being badly trimmed, and in particular by the sail

Spinnaker trim. RIGHT, TOP *Oversheeted — the spinnaker is too far round, the slot closed.* CENTRE *With the sheet eased, the spinnaker pulls the boat forward.* BOTTOM ROW *With the pole too far forward* (BELOW) *the luff and leech fall in together; with the pole too far back* (RIGHT) *the luff falls in and the foot is tight across the forestay.*

ABOVE *Broaching. The first sign of a broach is increased helm weight — control may be maintained by dumping the main traveller; dumping the mainsheet; dumping the kicker (to lift the boom end out of the water, as well as further depowering the mainsail); easing the spinnaker sheet. Sometimes, of course, it all happens rather quickly.*

being too full aloft. When this happens the top of the spinnaker starts to sway from side to side, pulling on first one side of the mast, then the other and acting like a giant pendulum.

As the wind strengthens the spinnaker has to be flattened to take some of the power out of its shoulders. This is done by leading the sheet and guy from progressively further forward, until they are both led through blocks almost up at the shrouds. In this way, the two corners of the sail are pulled down, narrowing and flattening the head of the sail.

Moving the leads. In lighter winds the leads are moved by clipping a block to the toe rail forward of the spinnaker sheet lead and pulling the sheet down and into the snatch block by brute force.

In stronger winds, however, brute force will not be enough and cunning must be used. The lazy guy and the lazy sheet are simple and ideal tools to use when moving spinnaker leads. Rig the new lead block for the spinnaker sheet in the desired position — using a snatch block — with another just ahead of it. Rig the lazy guy, which of course has no weight on it, through the forward block and take the weight of the sail on it, either on a free winch or direct to a cleat. Now let the weight right off the sheet, rig it through the new

K·511
K·511
K1000
K·1000
K1046

block, take the turns on the winch again and take the weight of the sail back onto the sheet. Finally take the lazy guy out of the move block.

The same technique can be used with the lazy sheet to move the lead of the guy.

Re-trimming the flatter sail. As the leads are moved forward, so the corners of the sail move downwards, requiring the pole to be lowered to keep the tack and clew at the same height. It can pay now to have the pole slightly forward of its normal setting, and to de-power the spinnaker by oversheeting. Too much power and the energy is used up in making the yacht roll.

Rules for reaching

The reaching spinnaker is flatter than the running spinnaker, either by virtue of different trimming technique and leads or by being a different sail (see chapter 9). For reaching the guy will normally be led forward, usually at the point of maximum beam of the yacht, while the sheet will lead from further aft. It is illegal under the racing rules to lead the sheet through the end of the main boom or through an outrigger.

Both the foot and the head of the sail must be flatter than for running to reduce the heeling moment; when shy reaching — that is with the apparent wind forward of the beam — the sail is acting more like a genoa than a running spinnaker.

Pole and tack height

When broad or beam reaching, tack and clew should be the same height (as for running) and this height will be dictated by the free-flying clew. As the apparent wind moves forward, the pole can be used to set the height of the corners of the sail and the clew made to follow.

Shy reaching, we want the tack of the sail low, to lengthen the apparent length of the luff — the projected length — and to straighten the luff and flatten

LEFT *Note the jockey pole on K-511.*

ABOVE *Rigging the jockey pole.*

the sail, again to lessen the heeling moment. The pole can be bowsed down on the foreguy (lowering the mast end to match) and the clew barber-hauled down to the required height.

Barber-hauling the spinnaker

There are two ways to do this. Either clip a snatch block over the sheet, with a line led from the block through another block on the toe rail (or a convenient dead eye on deck) to a winch. The sheet can be pulled downwards using this barber-haul, and pulled aft using the mainsheet winch. Another method is to use the lazy guy as the barber-hauler: lead the lazy guy through a snatch block on the toe rail, set just under or forward of the clew of the spinnaker, and pull the clew downwards with this, winching the lazy guy in on a spare winch.

The jockey pole

This is simply a short strut used as a bearing-out spar on the spinnaker when shy reaching. It is needed because on modern, wide yachts the spinnaker guy, even led from the point of maximum beam, bears hard against the shrouds when the pole is well forward.

Setting the jockey pole. The jockey pole is clipped to a fixed ring on the side of the mast, just above the level of the top guardrail. Clip on the pole with the outboard end passing out aft of the main shroud. A sail tie is usually used to lash the pole to the shroud, principally to hold it in place until the load comes on it from the guy. Nearly always the jockey pole is called for only when the guy is already up against the shrouds, but in whatever case, the pole should be underneath the guy.

The jockey pole has an open-ended sheave at its outer end, over which the spinnaker guy is to run. If there is not too much weight in the guy, it will be possible simply to push it out and into the jockey pole end, always remembering that this new lead is increasing the distance the guy travels between the spinnaker and the lead block, so simple geometry requires that the guy is eased as it is pushed out.

If there is too much weight on the guy for this you can use one of two methods.

1. Take the weight temporarily on the lazy sheet, ease the guy to get it in the pole end and then winch back again on the guy to take the weight back off the lazy sheet. Problems may arise with this method because the lead to the end of the spinnaker pole becomes even worse, albeit very briefly.
2. A better system is to lead the lazy sheet through the jockey pole sheave before taking the weight on it to allow the guy to be eased (if the sheet jams under the guy in the sheave it can easily be winched out).

These methods apply when the pole has to go aft of the main shroud. If, as on some yachts, the pole can sit *forward* of the main shroud simply clip it to the mast with the outboard end along the foredeck, put the sheave against the guy and then push the pole aft and thus the guy outwards. Tie it off to the main shroud.

8 · Gybing the spinnaker

Gybing the spinnaker should be a manoeuvre which holds no greater terror for the good crew than does tacking. The type of gear with which the yacht is fitted (see chapter 6) will to a great extent dictate the method by which the spinnaker is handled. With the double-ended pole both end-for-end gybes and dip-pole gybes are possible.

Double-ended pole: end-for-end gybe on the run

This is the method used with smaller spinnakers. The pole fittings at each end are identical; the pole is supported by a topping lift led to a wire span or bridle so that, held only by the topping lift, the pole would appear to hang on a sling. Single lines to the spinnaker are used, each line acting as both the sheet and the guy, depending on where the pole is.

In the end-for-end gybe, the pole in effect moves horizontally across the boat, the inboard end becoming the outboard end and vice versa.

Personnel

Two people are needed to look after the spinnaker, one on the foredeck and one in the cockpit who looks after both sheet and guy. In addition, there must be someone to gybe the mainsail and someone to look after the runners. There should be someone steering the yacht — no kidding, the helmsman is an important member of the gybing team. The boat should be steered as straight downwind as possible; it is particularly important not to luff up on the new gybe while the spinnaker is still being handled. The Golden Rule is: **keep her under the chute**.

The gybe least likely to go wrong is the gybe from one side to the other while square running or very broad reaching. Here is how it goes.

Foredeck

Before even going onto the foredeck, ensure that the pole is set at a height where it can be reached without climbing: ideally it should be at shoulder height. Then ease the downhaul slightly: not enough to allow the pole to go out of control, but enough to take the tension off it and the pole. The downhaul, when hard on, forces the pole end against the mast and if not eased before the gybe the pole, mast, downhaul and topping lift act like a giant bow and arrow so that the pole flies off the mast as soon as the catch is released. Even if this does not happen, the foredeck hand will have a very hard task pushing out against the downhaul to set the pole on the other gybe. So ease the downhaul before you start.

Once on the foredeck make sure the leeward genoa sheet is within easy reach, if necessary by holding it in the crook of your elbow. Stand at the mast, on the weather side, facing forwards. Many crews start to handle the pole standing in front of the mast facing aft: but they find halfway through the gybe they have to change position to complete the operation. If you work facing forwards, you are watching the spinnaker the whole time and are in greater control of what is happening.

Once the word 'go' is given, unclip the pole, move with it round the front of the mast and at the same time slip the slack genoa sheet over the end. Pull the pole (hanging on the topping-lift bridle, so there is no weight on it) across and grab the spinnaker sheet just forward of the shroud. Clip the pole upwards onto the spinnaker sheet (on all yacht spinnaker systems, the pole is used with the open jaw of the end fitting facing upwards) and continue pushing the pole out, at the same time sliding it forwards along what has now become the guy towards the corner of the spinnaker.

While doing this, pull the release line to the other

End for end gybe. (1) with the 'new' genoa sheet ready, stand at the mast <u>facing forwards</u>. Unclip the pole.

(2) Drop the genoa sheet over the pole end, pass the pole (hanging in the topping-lift sling) across the boat.

(3) Grab the new guy.

(4) Fit the guy into the pole end.

(5) Trip the other end, drop the old genoa sheet off.

(6) Clip on.

end of the pole and flick that end downwards, allowing what was the guy and is now the sheet to ride up clear of the pole. Make sure the genoa sheet has dropped off this end of the pole. Continue to push the pole across and clip it up into the ring on the mast. The spinnaker has been gybed.

In light weather. A smoother gybe results if, once the pole is unclipped from the mast, it is unclipped from the old guy before being clipped to the new guy. The spinnaker floats wide and clear without the danger of a collapse being brought on by the two corners being pulled together by the relatively short spinnaker pole. However, there comes a point, as the wind increases, where to do this is unsafe, as the spinnaker can take charge.

Meanwhile, Back Aft

With a simple run-to-run, end-for-end gybe it should not be necessary to touch the sheet and guy at all. The main should be gybed at the moment the inboard end of the pole is clipped onto the new guy, thus keeping the flow of air to the spinnaker as unimpeded as possible.

Runners. In light and medium winds release the old runner, and bring on the new runner just as the main comes across.

In heavy weather, pull the main in to the centreline, bring on the new runner, let off the old runner, gybe and then let the main out on the new side.

Note that it is always more important to let the old runner off than to pull the new one on: the boom must not hit the old runner as it swings across as this could carry away the entire rig.

Mainsail. The main can be pulled across by hand in light weather, but as the breeze increases it must be

BELOW End-for-end gybe, viewed from off the boat. Note how the spinnaker stays full throughout.

trimmed in on the sheet to close-hauled, gybed and then eased out on the sheet. Just when the change is made depends on the size of mainsail: on big mainsails, the sheet should always be used.

Double-ended pole: dip-pole gybe from reach to reach

Gybing from a reach to a reach the end-for-end method can be used, but as the reaches become shyer, greater difficulty is experienced in keeping everything under control and, in particular, in clipping the pole back onto the mast. Try the dip-pole gybe. For this, the mast end of the pole has to be on a track which allows it to ride up the front of the mast. It must go high enough to allow the outer end of the pole to swing down on the topping-lift bridle and come in under the forestay. The pole is then raised to horizontal by dropping the mast end to its former position.

Foredeck

Ease the downhaul, go forward. As the yacht bears away into the gybe, trip the guy out of the pole end by pulling the string, and at the same time hit the underside of the pole at the mast end hard with the heel of your hand. This will send the inboard end up the mast and capsize the pole, leaving it hanging in the topping-lift bridle so that the outboard end points down at the foredeck. Swing the end round behind the forestay (and in between the genoa sheets, to put the other one over the pole end) then pull down on the mast end to tip the pole back to horizontal.

As the yacht gybes, the spinnaker is trimmed to swing across the front of the forestay, bringing what will now be the guy to the pole end. Clip on. Move back aft and re-set the downhaul.

Meanwhile, Back Aft

The spinnaker trimmer is very important in this gybe. As the yacht gybes the spinnaker must be trimmed (hauling in the new sheet, easing away the new guy) to move the sail round to meet the pole end. In particular the new guy has to be over-eased, past its proper setting, to allow it to be clipped to the pole. Then it must be trimmed back to the correct setting. Make sure the foredeck hand has all the guy required.

Single-ended pole

By definition, a single-ended pole can only be gybed by the dip-pole technique, since the mast end always stays on the mast. Lazy sheets and guys are also always used. More elaborate preparation is required than for the simpler double-ended pole end-for-end gybe, and a bigger team is needed, since there are more jobs to be done and the gear is that much heavier.

Personnel

There must be:

- a foredeck hand, who works mainly in the pulpit;
- a mast hand, working at the mast;
- someone on the topping lift and foreguy;
- someone on the sheet and guy, each side (in light weather or smaller yachts, this can be one person doing both sides);
- someone on the runners, if fitted;
- someone on the mainsheet;
- and, of course, the helmsman.

Making ready

Let us not forget the 'four peas': Poor Preparation — Poor Performance.

The headsail, staysail or big boy must be handed and out of the way. It is a wise precaution to take one of the spare halyards, stowed on the mast, and clip it on the pulpit: this ensures that when the gybe is over, we do not end up with all the spare halyards on the wrong side of the spinnaker pole.

Take the genoa sheets off the genoa and tie them together. This keeps them led correctly over the pole, and they can be untied and reattached to the genoa when needed. The genoa should be pushed down out of the way of the pole end. The babystay must be unshipped and taken back to the mast, otherwise the spinnaker pole cannot swing across the foredeck.

The lazy guy (which is about to become the working

1

2

A dip-pole gybe, run to run. Trip the sail (1), dip the pole (2) and clip on the new guy (3). Raise the pole and gybe the main (4); winch the pole aft (5) and trim the sail (6).

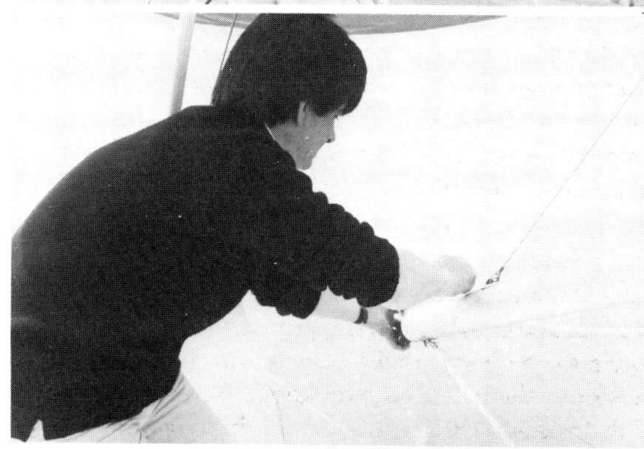
3

4

5

6

guy) should be pulled well forward into the pulpit, but led the way it will lead when working — there should not be any loops in it, to keep life simple in the hurried moments of the actual gybe.

Make sure that the lazy sheet is over the top of the pole end, so that the pole, when tripped, can swing freely downwards, away from the old guy.

Also check that a strop (usually a sail tie) has been rigged to the toggle on the tripping line of the pole, to enable it to be reached with the pole raised up the mast.

Finally, make sure everyone knows what they have to do: if necessary the crew boss should talk the whole operation through.

Foredeck

The foredeck hand should be positioned in the pulpit, ahead of the forestay, facing aft. The mast hand raises the inboard end of the pole on its track to the mark that indicates the pole end is high enough to allow the outboard end down and under the forestay; then trips the pole by pulling on the tripping line to open the jaw at the outboard end, releasing the guy. The spinnaker will lift the guy out and clear of the pole end.

The pulpit hand hauls in on the foreguy as the pole end is lowered on the topping lift. Guide the pole end down and under the forestay, dropping the unwanted genoa sheet off the end and slipping the new genoa sheet over the end as the pole comes through. As the pole swings under the forestay, call for the topping lift to raise the pole again, at the same time leading the new guy correctly through the jaw at the pole end and snapping the plunger closed — keeping your finger out of the way. Check to see there are no snags with the genoa sheet or the foreguy as the pole is topped up and the sail retrimmed.

The mast hand lowers the inboard end of the pole to the correct height for proper spinnaker trim.

This done, the two on the foredeck should gybe the genoa which is lying on deck by pulling it round the foreguy and leading it down the new leeward side, so that it is ready for hoisting if needed.

If the yacht is close reaching, the babystay must be set up again. It will now be on the wrong side of the pole, and have to be led over the topping lift.

Meanwhile, Back Aft

A good hand on the topping lift is vital, for a large part of the smooth gybe depends upon teamwork between the topping lift and the pulpit. The trimmers have the sheet and guy on each side, changing from 'lazy' to 'working' and 'working' to 'lazy' as the gybe progresses. Each must watch what is going on, and keep in step with the rest of the team: gybing is very much a team effort and the Golden Rule is **watch the others**.

Mainsail and runners. Treat exactly as dealt with earlier in this chapter, bearing in mind that the mainsail on this size of yacht will be too big to be handled casually: it must always be handled on the sheet. The main traveller should always be centred and cleated off — it should not be allowed to fly across the track unchecked. Sooner or later it just hits thed end-stop and keeps going.

Golden Rule: **Keep air in the spinnaker**. Trim the main amidships at the start of the gybe, then gybe the mainboom as the pole comes across. This keeps most of the spinnaker working in clear air and helps keep it full and flying. If the main is gybed late, it blankets the spinnaker which then collapses, causing all sorts of problems as it wraps itself round the head of the person in the pulpit and over the end of the pole.

9 · Changing the spinnaker

We now learn why the yacht is blessed with more than one spinnaker halyard: she carries anything up to five different spinnakers, each designed with a different task in mind, made from different weights of cloth and constructed in different ways.

The usual method of changing spinnakers on a racing yacht is the *peel*, developed, like most racing crewing techniques, to lose as little speed as possible during the work. Done perfectly, the peel will lose no speed at all, since in essence it involves setting the new spinnaker inside the existing spinnaker, getting the new sail drawing and then releasing the tack of the old sail so that it peels away from the swelling face of the new sail like a layer of onion skin to flutter briefly, flag-like, before being spirited away.

BELOW *Rigging a peeling strop.*

This is the simple inside hoist/outside drop, the classic peel — and sometimes it actually works like that, too.

Less neat is the opposite version, the outside hoist/inside drop, where the new sail goes up outside the old sail, is filled and got drawing and the old taken down inside the curve of the new sail. It seldom works like that, because as the new spinnaker goes up it tends to upset and collapse the old spinnaker, and it cannot really find the air to fill until the old sail is down and out of the way.

Why then ever do an outside hoist? The position of the halyards dictates which technique is employed, for the halyards must not be crossed at any stage during the change. So if the existing spinnaker is up on the windward halyard (spinnaker on starboard halyard with the boat on starboard gybe, or port halyard with the boat on port gybe), an outside (i.e. leeward) hoist has to be used.

Gear

Only one pole is used throughout the change, but we need a sheet and guy for the new spinnaker in addition to the sheet and guy on the spinnaker already flying. As sheet, we normally will use the lazy guy off the sail already set as a changing sheet, and to act as a temporary guy a short length of line with a spinnaker clip on the end is used. This is called a peeling strop.

Peeling strop. The peeling strop should be tied in the pulpit, usually to the stem-head fitting or to the forestay or headfoil itself. For this, use a rolling hitch so that the strop does not slide up the forestay. Hitch the strop to the forestay itself under the bottom piece of the headfoil, rather than round the headfoil if possible, to avoid the risk of crushing the headfoil. The

clip goes straight onto the spinnaker tack, led to weather of the forestay.

The length of the strop should be such as to allow the new spinnaker to set with the tack just above the height of the pulpit, but near the forestay. Once set, and with the old sail released, the guy will be pulled through the pole end to be clipped to the tack of the new sail, so this must be in easy reach of the crew member working in the pulpit.

Peeling

Let's take a simple situation as an example. The yacht is reaching along under the triradial on starboard gybe. The wind is showing signs of increasing in strength, and drawing ahead; already there has been one near broach as a stronger than usual gust came through. We decide to change to the slightly smaller starcut, which being flatter as well as smaller will be a better sail for these conditions. The triradial is set on the port halyard, so it will be an inside hoist/outside drop. We have the sheet and lazy guy rigged on the existing sail, with the guy and lazy sheet on the other (starboard) side.

Making ready

The new sail is brought on deck still packed in its turtle, the three corners ready for clipping on. Unclip the lazy guy from the clew of the existing spinnaker (help may be needed here to pull the sheet downwards and inboard, to allow the clips to be reached). Clip on the lazy guy as sheet to the new sail.

Take the tack of the new sail forward to the peeling strop already hitched to the forestay and clip on.

Unclip the starboard spinnaker halyard from its stowed position (probably on the mast) and check its lead, visualising how the head of the sail will travel aloft when the time comes to hoist. If the halyard has been stowed normally, it will have to be taken forward and round the forestay, so that it leads over the top of the forestay, before being brought aft and clipped to the new spinnaker. We are ready to go.

Peeling spinnakers (1). LEFT The new spinnaker is set up on the bow, the halyard cleared and clipped on. BELOW The new spinnaker is hoisted, the tack held by the strop.

Personnel

To peel the spinnaker we will need:

- someone on the halyards, to pull the new sail up and secure the halyard, then let the old halyard go to lower the old sail;
- someone on the sheets (port side) to set the new sail and to throw the sheet of the old sail off the winch;
- people to gather in the old sail;
- someone on the guy (starboard side) to ease the pole forward to where the foredeck hand can release the guy, and to let the guy on forward to collect the new sail;
- possibly someone on the topping lift to ensure that the pole is low enough for the foredeck hand to reach everything.

Peeling spinnakers (2). The old spinnaker is tripped (BELOW); the guy is taken to the new spinnaker (RIGHT).

Foredeck

The foredeck hand has a busy time during a peel. You must:

- make the new spinnaker ready and clip it on;
- move back to the mast to hand-haul the spinnaker halyard to hoist the new sail, while the tailer takes the halyard up on the winch;
- move forward and possibly climb up in the pulpit to release the tack of the old sail, then pull the guy through the pole end to the new sail;
- then move aft again to help gather in the old sail as it comes down.

The hoist

When all is ready the new spinnaker is hoisted smartly, the foredeck hand hauling on the halyard at the mast, the tailer tacking the halyard onto the winch. Once the sail is up, the sheet is taken in until the sail fills and begins to set. With the tack of the sail on the peeling strop, there is nothing for the guy hand to do, until . . .

The changeover

With the new sail up, let the pole go forward until the

foredeck hand can release the tack of the old sail. The guy must now be eased further, so that the foredeck hand can take it down and clip it to the tack of the new sail. When the guy is clipped on, the foredeck hand calls aft and unclips the peeling strop, and the guy hand hauls in the guy to bring the tack to the pole, then trims the pole to where it should be.

The drop

As the old sail flags out, the old sheet must be hauled in from as far forward as possible, the foot of the sail gathered and the halyard let go for the old sail to be gathered. Handing the spinnaker is dealt with fully in the next chapter, which if nothing else demonstrates the wisdom of reading the whole book before trying any of the individual moves described.

Meanwhile, Back Aft

Yet again, it is teamwork which counts and we have already seen how the action shifts quickly from the foredeck to the cockpit and back again. Everyone must watch everyone else and stay with what is going on.

Of those back aft, the guy hand in particular is crucial to the slickness of the operation, having to let the pole forward by the right amount at the right moment, pause while the foredeck hand releases the old sail, then let the guy on forward so that the foredeck hand can attach it to the tack of the new sail.

Variations

Outside hoist. As mentioned earlier, the position of the halyards dictates which technique is used. Had the triradial in our example been up on the starboard halyard, the starcut would have had to go up on the port halyard. In this case the port halyard would be taken from its stowage on the mast, the lead checked aloft, the halyard led outside the sheet of the triradial and back over the top of the guardrail to the head of the starcut.

With an outside hoist, the pole should be let forward right to the forestay before the old sail is released; this will prevent it blowing out round the luff of the new sail before it can be lowered.

Doing without the peeling strop. When there is already a lazy sheet rigged along with the guy through the pole end, it is sometimes neater to do without the peeling strop, and take the lazy sheet direct to the new sail for temporary use as the new guy.

The disadvantage is that it takes longer to prepare: the pole end is often out of reach, and must be brought within reach to get the lazy sheet off the existing sail. The weight of the existing sail must briefly be taken on the lazy sheet so that the guy can be unclipped from the ring on the sheet and clipped direct to the sail, then the weight taken back on the guy to unclip and pull through the lazy sheet. This chore can interfere with the setting of the existing spinnaker, but once the lazy sheet is in hand we have plenty of benefits to outweigh this disadvantage.

The lazy sheet is led to the tack of the new sail, and on hoisting the tack of the new sail is pulled out to the pole end before the old sail is released. (Indeed, if this is done, there is no need to do any climbing to release the old sail: just let the guy go completely and gather it on the foredeck, to be pulled back when the sail is out of the way.)

This method has great advantage when peeling with the wind well aft, since it gets the new spinnaker out into clear air very quickly. When doing an outside hoist/inside drop it both allows the new spinnaker to set more quickly and greatly simplifies handing the old spinnaker.

Bare-headed changing

Not every spinnaker change has to be done by peeling. It is sometimes better to take one spinnaker off before putting the next one up: the only criterion being which method will lose the yacht the least speed. In heavy weather something going wrong can lose a great deal of time, even if it does not become actually dangerous; with the boat going at near her maximum speed under mainsail alone anyway, it

Peeling spinnakers (3). The old spinnaker is handed (OPPOSITE).

K 5370

ABOVE The lightest member of the crew can be sent aloft in a bosun's chair to uncross the halyards.

might be both safer and ultimately quicker to hand one spinnaker before replacing it with another.

In very light weather, the inevitable disturbance of peeling, even with everyone creeping about on tiptoe and conversing in whispers, might slow the boat more than the brief loss of speed from a bare-headed change.

Uncrossing the halyards

In the course of a long, dark and fickle night, with two or three watch changes, there might routinely be two or three spinnaker peels; on one of those sloppy, frustrating nights that make you wonder what's so wrong with spending the night in bed there might be many more. Sooner or later it is realised that the halyards have become crossed, usually by using the wrong ploy.

The halyard is uncrossed by leading it outside the spinnaker which is up. Because of the shape of the sail at the top (where it will be almost horizontal) and because of the great belly of cloth beneath this horizontal top, this is a tricky business. The first question to ask is "can we safely leave it?"

If the next mark is close ahead, with a beat to follow, and the spinnaker that's up can be got down (possibly with having to let both halyards go), the answer is "yes", and the mess can be sorted out much more easily without a sail in the way. If the answer is "no", the halyard has to be retrieved.

A light line is attached to the working end of the halyard, and the halyard led forward to go round outside the sail. Take the line aft along the bottom of the sail and try pulling the halyard round. On no account force it, for the risk of snagging and tearing the spinnaker is great. If it won't come with the sail full, try collapsing the sail briefly by letting out the sheet very quickly, pulling the line as the sail flaps. This might sound drastic, but the sail need be collapsed only momentarily and eight times out of ten the halyard will fall freely past the sail.

The other two times are when there is more than one cross in the halyards. Here, the simplest solution might be to go up and get the halyard. Rig the bosun's chair and send the lightest crew member aloft. Up there, apart from having a fabulous view, the halyard can be pulled up and through the cross and the end dropped back down again with a clear lead.

This might sound drastic — but in the end it can prove the quickest method and less detrimental to speed than the ongoing distraction of a full-fledged committee meeting on the foredeck while assorted pet theories are tried and discarded.

10 · Handing the spinnaker

Before the spinnaker is taken off it is necessary to decide what is going to happen next (yacht races are won by thinking ahead) — so the correct headsail must be set before the spinnaker is handed. There is another, more prosaic, reason for setting the headsail: it is a great deal easier to get the spinnaker down behind the shelter of the headsail, than to get it down while it is still full of wind. The required headsail may be anything from the high-clewed reacher to the number three genoa: it should be brought on deck and any other headsail (left over from the previous leg) cleared away.

Basic rules for handing the spinnaker

There are several methods of handing the spinnaker, but all have a common aim: to transform that mighty, controlled giant, harmless enough when under control and pulling like a steam loco, into an equally harmless pile of empty, and preferably dry, nylon, safely below deck; and to do it with the minimum of fuss and in the shortest possible time. The longer the time taken over this transformation, the greater the chance of something going wrong.

The first Golden Rule of spinnaker handing is **get the wind out of it**; the second Golden Rule is **don't drop it, bring it down**.

The halyard

Of all the jobs in spinnaker handing, that of the person on the halyard is the most crucial, not just in terms of speed but also safety. Never let the halyard go until you can see where the sail will end up, no matter who is screaming at you. Usually the halyard is on the winch with four turns: in all but very big spinnakers it can be held by hand with three, maybe two. When it is called for, surge it round the winch with the turns still on; throw off one turn and make sure the others have the sail before you let it go completely. The Golden Rule is **do not let the sail go in the water**. If it does, most likely the speed of the boat will cause the whole sail to go overboard. The situation can be retrieved if the halyard hand acts quickly; hold the halyard on the winch or even haul it back to let them pull the sail from the water.

If the worst happens and the whole sail is in the water and the boat still moving, it may be necessary to cut the halyard to stop the sail acting like a trawl and let it empty of water, so that it can be recovered.

Conventional cockpit drop

The standard, the easiest and probably the safest method.

The spinnaker pole is let forward until the tack is within reach; the clip between the guy and the tack is released and the spinnaker flutters out like a flag behind the mainsail, held by the halyard and the sheet; the sheet is hauled in to reach the clew; the foot of the sail is gathered in so the sail resembles a long ribbon; the sail is lowered on the halyard and bundled down through the main hatch.

Personnel

We need:

- someone on the guy, to let the pole forward;
- someone on the foredeck, to trip (release) the sail;
- someone on the sheet, to start gathering the sail;
- someone on the halyard, to lower the sail.

Method

Set the new headsail and trim it on the sheet (even if

1

2

3

it will not set properly, have the sheet trimmed in; a flapping or loose headsail will merely get in the way of handing the spinnaker). *Ease the pole* forward so that the foredeck hand can reach the pole end and the trip line to the spinnaker clip on the guy.

The foredeck hand may have to climb up in the pulpit if the pole has been carried high — on a medium-air run, for example — or it may be necessary to lower the pole end on the topping lift.

The foredeck hand *trips the sail* by releasing the clip — most types work with a trip line. On bigger yachts, the clip may be of the type with a trigger: use a hardwood or metal spike to release the clip, *not* your finger.

Golden Rule: **mind your head**. Even on a small yacht, the load on the spinnaker guy can be enough to cause the pole to whip back aft as the sail is released, cracking the skull or splitting open the eyebrow of anyone foolish enough to have their head in the way. Similarly, the corner of the sail can flick with the viciousness of a whip as it flies free, so keep head and face below the pole as the sail is released.

As the sail flags out behind the mainsail, haul in the sheet to grab the clew and *gather the foot*, pulling in along the foot tape (usually white) until both corners of the sail are to hand.

Let go the halyard, pulling the falling sail inboard under the boom and bundling it as quickly as possible down the hatch and out of the way.

It is *vital* to gather the foot of the sail before letting go the halyard. With practice and teamwork, corners can be cut and the spinnaker spirited away in one slick, flowing movement — but even then the foot of the sail must be under control and coming inboard more quickly than the head of the sail can fall. If the halyard is let go with the sail still half full of wind, it is virtually certain that some of the sail will fall in the water. At best this slows the handing of the sail, it can also slow the boat, and at worst it spells virtual disaster.

4

5

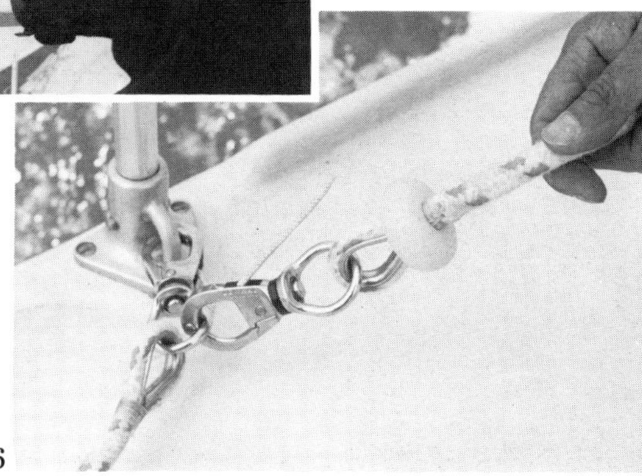

6

The basic cockpit drop. Trip the guy (1), keeping your head down; gather the foot (2) then gather the luffs and lower the sail (3), keeping the halyard under control. Unclip the halyard (4) and clip it back on the mast. Take off the pole (5), lead the guy around the forestay and take the sheet forward. Clip the sheet and guy together and to their stowage point (6).

True story

A 51-footer is running fast towards the downwind mark; she has a good lead and the crew are enjoying themselves, working well together and being very slick. A straight cockpit drop is called, but before the foot of the sail is properly inboard, the halyard is flung off. The top of the sail goes in the water with the yacht still doing nine knots; it fills; it starts dragging the rest of the sail in. Two men are pulled off their feet before they can let go; a third, caught up by the sail, is flicked up, out and overboard like a rag doll. The spinnaker, now a water-filled drogue, slews the boat around into a crash gybe; only prompt action by the man on the runner saves the mast but the boom, slamming across the deck like a barn door in a gale, catches the mainsheet trimmer across the shoulders and topples him, breathless, over the guardrails into the water on the opposite side to the first man overboard.

Both men were recovered, indignant but otherwise unhurt, and even the spinnaker was retrieved at only the cost of a cut halyard, but it was a very subdued crew who took the boat up the final beat and back to her berth; they did not win. Slower is usually safer.

Organisation

On a big boat, there will usually be at least one person for each job, plus a couple of spare hands to gather in the sail. On a small boat (say with only four in the crew counting the helmsman), some people will have to do more than one job.

- The hand on the guy eases the pole forward, then goes across to help gather the sail;
- the foredeck hand trips the sail from the pole, then moves aft to the halyard;
- the sheet hand starts hauling sheet as soon as the sail is tripped, and is joined by the guy hand;

- the foredeck hand lets go the halyard once the other two have the sail safely under the lee of the mainsail;
- the foredeck hand backs up on recovering the sail once the halyard no longer needs tending, to relieve the guy hand who then attends to the mainsheet as the yacht reaches the mark and starts to harden up, while the sheet hand looks after the genoa.

Foredeck drop from reaching

The sail is brought down behind and under the genoa, to be gathered on the foredeck and (usually but not necessarily) bundled straight down the forehatch. The tack of the sail is not let go completely but instead the guy is let go and the tack pulled in and down behind the genoa using the lazy sheet or a line rigged specially for the purpose: this collapses the sail at the luff and the sheet is dumped to empty the sail. With this method, it is the luff which must be pulled down first and quickest; the sheet can even be held to keep the foot taut and inside the rail.

Personnel

Much as for the cockpit drop. On a boat with a big spinnaker an extra person will be needed on the foredeck to gather the sail, and on yachts over 36 ft someone usually goes below the open forehatch, to act as long stop on the lazy sheet or recovery line, and to gather the sail as it is bundled through the hatch.

Method

On a yacht with single guy and sheet, fasten a spare length of line, heavy enough to be handled under load without cutting hands, to the tack of the sail. Lead this forward and round the forestay to leeward of the genoa, over the top of and inside the pulpit and guardrails and under the foot of the genoa. Secure the end to something substantial, like the mast. Alternatively you can use the lazy sheet (if there is one), either by unreeving it from the lead blocks aft or by taking a bight forward, if there is enough line: make sure there is plenty of slack in the lazy sheet to bring it well back on the foredeck.

On the word to hand the sail, ease the guy forward until the pole is on the forestay, the foredeck hand taking in the slack on the lazy sheet or retrieval line. When the pole is on the forestay, keep the guy going out, fast but sensibly, until all the weight is transferred; at the same time the foredeck hand or team hauls in on the retrieval line. Once they have the weight, the guy hand throws the guy right off the winch and makes sure it is clear to be pulled through. This should all happen a good deal faster than the time it takes to read about it.

As the tack comes in behind and under the genoa, the luff of the spinnaker pulls taut, backfills and the sail collapses. If it does not collapse immediately, the sheet hand should dump the sheet, but not let it go. Hold the foot taut and clear of the water as the halyard is let go.

The halyard should be let go just as the weight comes on the retrieval line and the tack starts to come under the genoa, but not while there is still wind in the sail, otherwise the sail goes in the water.

The sheet can finally be let go once the spinnaker is coming in under the genoa, so that foot and the upper part of the luff are handed together, while the sheet hand trims the genoa sheet.

Advantages. This is a very fast method when done correctly, and by bringing the sail down behind the

Foredeck drop on the reach (ABOVE) The lazy sheet or retrieval line is brought under the genoa and the guy let go. Pull like fury and bundle the sail down the hatch.

genoa, the drop can be left much later. If a cockpit drop is left too late and the yacht hardens up round the mark, the spinnaker is carried aft and out from the lee of the main and is real trouble to get down. With a foredeck drop it is almost an advantage to leave everything late, for the spinnaker falls behind both genoa and main and is virtually blown inboard by the flow of air building up across the back of the genoa as the yacht comes on the wind.

The pole can stay up, safe against the forestay, as the yacht rounds up round the mark, to be taken down later (thus saving precious seconds).

This method can only be used when leaving the mark to the windward side; leaving the mark to leeward — and thus having to gybe round it — an early drop or a full float drop has to be used.

Foredeck drop from running

Use the same method of bringing the spinnaker down, but instead of bringing it in to leeward under the genoa, bring the retrieval line or bight of the lazy sheet straight down onto the deck from the end of the squared-off pole, and thus bring the sail in to weather of the forestay and genoa.

Method

Ease the guy to transfer the weight to the retrieval line, and at the same time dump the sheet completely to empty the sail — which would otherwise remain full, tacked not to the guy on the pole but to the poor guy on the foredeck (this is illegal, as well as being hard work). The halyard can be let go allowing the sail to fall onto the foredeck — the boat virtually sails underneath the falling spinnaker — but take care that the sail does not fall over the bow and into the water, to be run down by the boat. That really slows things up.

BELOW We're only here for the cod. If the spinnaker goes in the water, gather it aboard by pulling one tape at a time to spill water from the sail.

drop

A float drop is simply taking the pole off and putting it away before taking the spinnaker down, leaving the spinnaker to float free and continue drawing while this is done. It can thus only be done square or very broad to the wind. It is quite legal provided there is no untoward delay in handing the spinnaker once the pole is stowed. A float drop is often used in light weather when no gybe is involved. But in any wind strength it is very useful if a gybe drop is needed, in other words if the mark has to be left to leeward.

Float drop in light weather, no gybe

Simply remove the pole by tripping it away from the guy, taking it off the mast and stowing it. On boats with small spinnakers this is a one-person operation, on bigger boats it needs the foredeck hand to trip the pole, plus someone to tend the topping lift. As for gybing, make sure the lazy sheet is over the end of the pole before tripping, or the pole cannot fall away free when the topping lift is eased. The sail can either be brought down to windward or to leeward.

Float drop and gybe

Now we are becoming quite ambitious, although this method is much less complicated to do than to describe. It is also impressive to watch — but more important, it pays big dividends in time saved at the mark.

It is used when approaching the mark on a run with the mark to be left to leeward, involving a gybe round the mark. Simply, the pole is taken off and stowed, the spinnaker allowed to float free, the yacht gybed and the spinnaker handed on to the foredeck on what is the weather side after the gybe.

Method. Take the pole off and stow it. Gybe the main *and the genoa*: the foredeck hand will have to help the genoa across and the genoa sheet hand must sheet it in to get it out of the way and ready for rounding up round the mark, which should now be mere feet away. The foredeck hand grabs what is now the lazy sheet (i.e. the slack rope to the spinnaker on the new weather side) and hauls it in, pulling the tack of the sail down to the deck at the mast and collapsing the sail from the luff. The sheet and lazy guy are let run completely to dump the spinnaker, which briefly flags out ahead of the forestay as the foot is gathered. At the same time, the halyard is thrown off the winch to let the sail fall onto the foredeck. The yacht is meanwhile rounding the mark, hardening up and so the spinnaker is blown into the weather side of the genoa which acts as a keep net, allowing the sail to come down onto the foredeck without going into the water.

Trimming with the pole off. Trimming with the pole off is essentially the same as trimming with it on, except that the guy may have to be trimmed in

(aft) to compensate for the distance the tack will move inboard when the pole is taken away. Obviously, this technique can only be used when running: if used when reaching, the spinnaker tack heads for the masthead as soon as it is released from the pole (bad news for those who like life on an even keel).

String take-down

This is a technique borrowed by big boats from dinghies, where a retrieval line (the string) is used to pull the spinnaker into a spinnaker chute. Big boats do not have spinnaker chutes, but the method is the same. It can only properly be used for a mark rounding leaving the mark to windward, i.e. without a gybe.

ABOVE *KC34675 ('Charisma') has approached the leeward mark on the rounding gybe, and goes for a late and fast string take-down, leaving the pole up until she is round and on the wind. 'Dihard' comes in on the other gybe and prepares for a late float drop; she will take off the pole, gybe the main and genoa and drop the spinnaker to starboard (i.e. to leeward) of the genoa. Note the genoa sheet over the pole; the foredeck hand is holding the port-side lazy guy to pull the spinnaker round and down as the manoeuvre gets under way. In a moment, things are going to get very busy on 'Dihard'.*

OPPOSITE *A float drop on the run. Take the pole off first and bring the spinnaker down to windward of the forestay.*

The string

The 'string' is a retrieval line (somewhat stronger, we hope, than mere string) attached to a patch on the front of the spinnaker at two-thirds height and led through a loop on the front of the spinnaker at one-third height. On smaller spinnakers, the loop is dispensed with and the patch is about half-height. For the drop, the string is led over the guardrail, under the genoa foot to the foredeck, just forward of the mast.

How it works

The pole goes on to the forestay as the yacht hardens round the mark. Sheet and guy are trimmed all the time until the spinnaker collapses because the yacht has come too close to the wind. The sheet and guy are held, keeping the foot taut, as the halyard is thrown off (and not merely eased or let go — it really must be dumped). At that instant, the string is pulled, fast. The sail comes down and the sheet and guy are released to allow the foot to be gathered.

How to make it work

The string should be outside the sail, to help it gather — much like the brail on an old-fashioned barge or square-rigger (truly, there is little new in seafaring). The foot must be kept taut until the rest of the sail is inboard. Speed is the secret of success. The halyard has to be flung off and the string pulled at the same instant. The head of the sail, with the yacht almost hard on the wind, does not fall downwards but rather blows away to leeward and the string gathers the sail so quickly that it does not have time to reach the water.

Clearing up

Once the spinnaker is down and out of the way, there are several chores which must be done instantly, if not sooner.

- Unclip the halyard, the sheets and guys. The halyard should be stowed back on the mast, making sure that the lead from the halyard sheave at the top of the mast to the stowage clip is fair and the halyard has not caught around anything, like the upper spreader.
- Put the sheets and guys back on their stowage hooks up forward. Do not put them on opposite hooks — put them on the same hook, with one set led around the forestay. That way, time will be saved when next the spinnaker is needed: if they are on the wrong side when the next hoist comes, it is a simple matter to clip them together and haul them round.
- Secure the pole in its stowage, stow the topping lift back on the mast. Haul taut the foreguy, to help secure the forward end of the pole.
- Set up the babystay, if fitted.

Ready to tack?

As quickly as possible, ensure that the yacht is clear to tack. In particular this means checking the weather genoa sheet, to make sure it has not been trapped under the pole, or left inside the babystay when that was clipped back on. If the genoa now up is not the one that came down when the spinnaker was set, check that the sheet lead position on the weather side is correct.

Packing the spinnaker

Always re-pack the spinnaker as soon as it comes off: never leave it. A sudden windshift, the discovery by the navigator that you've just rounded the wrong mark — anything might conspire to mean that it will be needed again without warning.

Turtle pack. Most spinnakers are now set flying, from a specially shaped bag called a turtle. The turtle has an especially wide mouth, probably with the edges stiffened by a wire hoop, and a fabric top which closes over the mouth like a lid. Some have three flaps, kept closed by Velcro, but the purpose of all is to keep the sail close-bagged until the moment the halyard is hauled.

A spinnaker can be packed by one person, but a big sail is more easily packed by two. Always start with the head.

1. Hook up the head. (Most serious racing yachts have a hook or two on a bulkhead below, or the

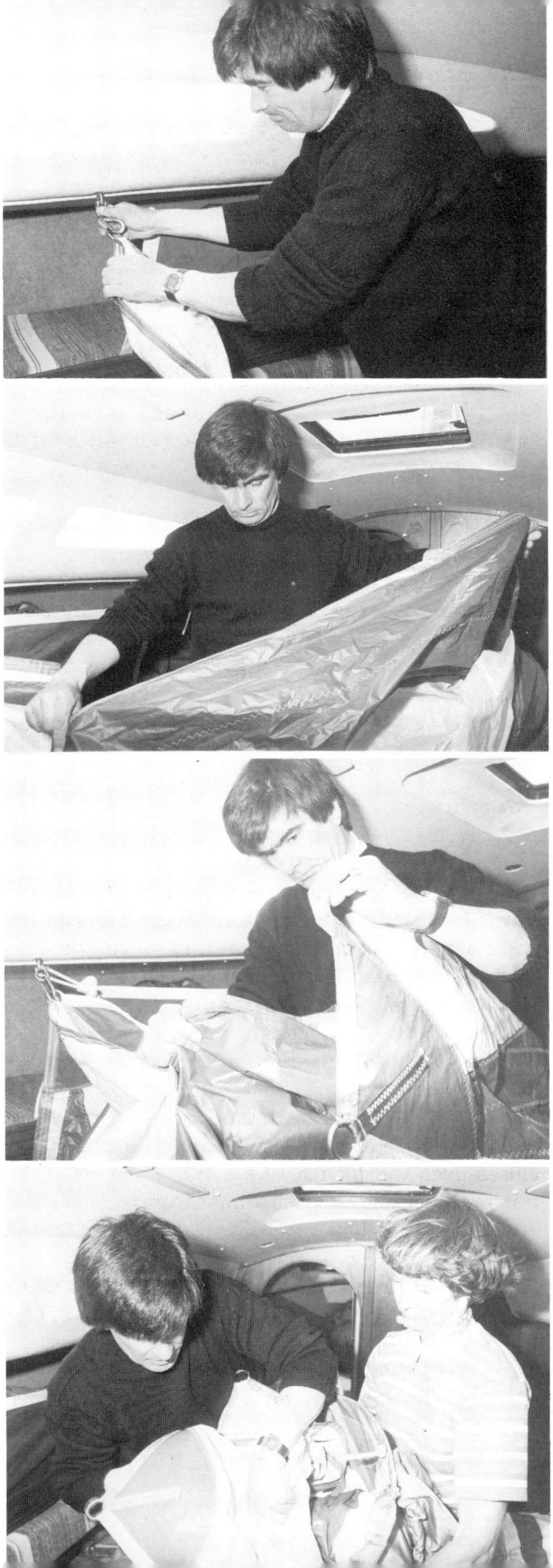

stump end of a deckhead grab handle might be used.)

2· From the head, follow down each of the luff tapes towards the clews, pulling the twists out of the sail until the clew comes to hand.
3· Hook up each clew.
4· Follow along the foot tape, to make doubly sure that there are no twists in the sail.
5· From the head, gather up each luff tape between fingers and thumb until the whole sail is hanging with the corners and edges uppermost, the bunt of the sail in a pile below.
6· Start pushing the sail into the turtle, from the middle of the bunt and working first towards the foot, then back towards the head, leaving the tapes and corners to last.
7· Pack the foot tape, leaving the two clews hanging over the edge of the turtle, then pack the top of the sail.
8· Fold the three corners into the turtle to lie on top of the packed sail, the head with the clews.
9· Clip or tie the three corners together using the top spring hook of the turtle, or the drawstring. This stops the corners becoming lost in the rest of the

LEFT Packing the spinnaker (see text). BELOW The packed sail should have the head and clews on top.

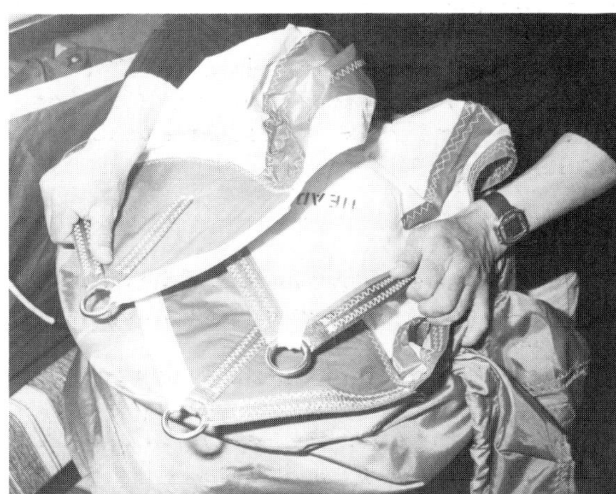

When to use what

In reverse order of difficulty, here is a guide:

Mark to be left to windward side of yacht

String take-down. If well practised beforehand, and only if the spinnaker has a string!

Windward foredeck drop. If approaching on a run in medium or light airs.

Leeward foredeck drop. Any time except very light airs (upsets the genoa trim too much).

Float drop. Light airs.

Cockpit drop. Any time.

Mark to leeward

Float drop and gybe. Any time except heavy weather.

Cockpit drop. Any time, but early. Do not forget to lower the forward end of the pole to let the genoa gybe.

Golden Rule: **safest is usually quickest.**

sail. Some turtles have lids designed to allow the three corners to protrude, held secure by a Velcro fastening.

As can be seen, this is all best done either by two people or one person with four arms. One person with only two arms can safely omit step five.

Setting in stops. Large spinnakers, or those which will be set in heavy weather, are sometimes set in stops. These are simply ties of wool or light cotton, or most usually light elastic bands, tied around the sail every few feet to prevent it filling on its way to the masthead. The sail is fully hoisted in its stops, looking like a long sausage or loosely woven nylon rope. When it is up and out at the pole end, the sheet is hauled to pull the clews apart. The sail fills from the bottom upwards, opening like a huge flower as the stops break.

You will need a large plastic bucket with the bottom cut out, and plentiful supply of elastic bands.

1· Fit a couple of dozen elastic bands over the outside of the bottomless bucket.
2· Hook up the head, and follow through the luff tapes to untwist the sail, as if packing in the normal way.
3· Pass the spinnaker, head first and with the luff tapes together, through the bucket, slipping the elastic bands over the sail at intervals of two feet or so.
4· With the sail stopped, coil it into the turtle from the foot, but leaving the foot itself (with the clews stopped together) over the edge of the turtle so that sheet and guy can be clipped on.

11 · Other downwind delights

There is a variety of sails which may be set along with the spinnaker, but one Golden Rule applies to all: **don't let it slow you down**. Too often, crews become carried away with piling on canvas, are distracted from trimming the canvas already set, and actually lose speed instead of gaining it.

Staysail

Staysails work inside the spinnaker, partly by increasing sail area, thus drive, but mostly by creating an extra slot ahead of the mainsail, increasing the flow of air across the face of the main and, to a lesser degree, across the inside of the spinnaker.

Blooper

The blooper or 'big boy' is a sail for square running, usually used on masthead-rig boats. It is set from the bow and on the opposite side to the spinnaker — it works by providing extra pull, and also balances the spinnaker, making the boat easier to steer. However, it is a tricky sail to make work and often does more harm than good — it has been nicknamed the Lunch Wrecker, which says a great deal about it. As well as causing distraction, the blooper can physically slow the boat if carried other than square before the wind, by causing greater heel and greater leeway. So always watch the speedo when playing around with bloopers and staysails.

Setting the blooper

Halyard. If the spinnaker is up on the windward halyard, the spare spinnaker halyard can be used, otherwise the leeward genoa halyard is used. The blooper is never gybed, rather handed and re-set if the yacht is gybed, so on three-halyard boats the genoa halyard is favourite. On handing the sail to gybe, take the halyard forward to the pulpit, so it is on the right side of the pole on the other gybe.

Sheet. A single sheet is used, usually left permanently bent on the sail. The sheet should be fairly light, so as not to drag the sail down by its weight, but thick enough not to burn the hands of the person handling.

RIGHT The blooper going up outside the spinnaker sheet.

LEFT Perfect blooper trim. The tack on its strop is just clear of the pulpit; the foot is parallel with the sea, the halyard and sheet eased off to keep the sail as far away from everything as possible. In trimming the blooper the halyard must be tended continually to keep the foot at the correct height.

Sheet winch. Use a spare winch on the leeward side, probably the spinnaker winch since the spinnaker sheet can go on the primary. Handling the blooper sheet without a winch usually results in rope-burned hands.

Tack strop. Usually kept on the sail, the tack strop is needed to carry the tack of the sail clear of the bow, to get the sail out into the clear air beyond the mainsail.

Making ready

Bring the sail in its bag to the lee side of the foredeck, at the rail. Lead the sheet aft and outboard of the shrouds, the spinnaker sheet and the mainsheet. Lead the halyard — the leewardmost halyard available — over the top of and outboard of the spinnaker sheet and lazy guy, back inboard over the rail and clip it to the head of the sail. Lead the tack strop and with it the tack forward, over the top of the rail to the stemhead, leading it outboard of the pulpit.

Personnel

For hoisting, we need:

- someone on the sheet;
- someone on the halyard at the winch;
- someone on the halyard at the mast;
- someone on the foredeck, to see the sail aloft and keep it out of the water.

ABOVE *'Scarlett O'Hara' with spinnaker staysail set under her triradial. Note the staysail tacked to the weather toe rail, 5 ft aft of the pulpit; the high clew; the staysail sheet led to a snatch block on the leeward toe rail; the staysail is set flying. The staysail is made from ultralight film cloth.*

Hoisting

Haul on the halyard at the mast, to pull the sail to about three-quarters height of the full hoist. As the sail comes out of the bag the foredeck hand must stop it falling into the water, then take the foot and tack in hand until the sail finds the wind and starts to lift. The sheet hand must tweak the sheet to flick the sail full: it is rather like getting a kite to fly.

Trimming

Trimming the blooper is a two-person job: one on the sheet, one on the halyard. Give the sail as much sheet as it will take: the further away from the boat and the mainsail it flies, the better. Once the sail has found the wind, lower the halyard until the flat part of the foot of the sail, near the tack, is flying parallel to the water. The halyard can be secured on the winch, but someone must stay at the mast to overhaul the halyard if the sail begins to drop, to keep the sail out of the water.

Heavy weather running

If no 'bullet-proof' heavy-weather running spinnaker is carried, downwind speed is sometimes maintained by using the spinnaker pole to boom out the clew of the genoa, thus balancing the main. Because of the limitation on the length of the spinnaker pole, the foot of the heavy number one will be too long, and the number three is often used.

A better idea is to set the number two, or even the heavy number one, as if it were a spinnaker, with the tack of the sail, held by the guy, out at the pole end and the sail set outside the forestay and sheeted in the normal spinnaker manner.

This is very fast, and very safe. The sail is cut flat compared with a spinnaker — which is what we want in heavy weather — and the widest part of the sail is much lower than it is with a spinnaker, thus keeping rolling to a minimum. There is much more control over a genoa set this way than over a boomed-out genoa.

12 · Around the course

So far, we have broken crewing down into a series of basic jobs: setting the spinnaker, changing the headsail, loading a winch. These are the chores of crewing, the basic skills which have to be learned before we become working members of the team. Just as you have to learn to beat eggs before you can make a cake, so you have to learn to pack a spinnaker before you can take on a yacht race. Beaten eggs and packed spinnakers are not especially meritorious examples of human achievement when viewed in isolation, however: they are merely small parts of a greater whole. Seldom in a yacht race do we do one job and then go back to bed. One job flows into the next: we change the headsail, then trim it, then tack the yacht and so on, and throughout, sail trimming is a continuing preoccupation. So all these skills are combined to sail the yacht round the course, and there should be no job on board which, when the need arises for it, fills the crew with horror and the thought "can't do that yet, haven't learned how to!"

Eight o'clock on race day

Eight o'clock on race day and the crew are assembling on the pontoon, while around them in the marina other cars and crews are arriving and other yachts are making ready.

The boat is opened up and bags are chucked on board, feet cleaned and the crew climb on board, the engine is started, the berthing lines let go and the yacht slides stern first out of her berth, her owner or sailing master at the helm, and turns her head towards the mouth of the river and the day's racing.

First things first: somebody puts the kettle on and gets a brew-up going.

Usually, marinas being what they are, the first job is to rig all the movable gear that was stowed in safety below at the end of the previous outing. The strop, the lead blocks and the snatch blocks come up and are rigged or stowed in their appropriate places. The navigator has the details of the course and the weather forecast and the latter is checked against the day to see if it bears any relation to reality. To give the forecasters their due, they are correct more often than not.

As the yacht motors to the start, the main cover comes off, the sail goes up and the first genoa of the day is prepared. On the way to the start is the time to talk any new crew member round the boat or, with several new members, time should have been made for at least a spinnaker gybe to let everyone find their place.

Arriving with plenty of time — an hour is not at all too much, and half-an-hour is the minimum — the yacht is taken up the first beat for fifteen minutes to try the headsail and let the navigator ponder the frequency of the wind oscillations. Back to the line and this is checked to find the bias. Maybe now we drop the headsail on deck and look at the others still sailing, sussing-out where we want to start.

Ten minutes to go

Ten minutes to go, and the headsail goes back up, the engine left running but out of gear in case it is needed for a last-minute dash to the other end of the line. The sailing beforehand has let the newcomers settle in and everyone knows what they are supposed to be doing. Sheets port and starboard, grinding and tailing; someone on the runners; someone up in the pulpit to watch for opposite-tack yachts (in particular, starboard-tack yachts!); someone at the mast, to help the genoa round in the tacks. The navigator is by the helmsman, calling the time to the start, watching for signals from the committee vessel.

ABOVE Clear wind and speed are vital just after the start. The crew must provide the helmsman with the fastest boat in the fleet by trimming for power.

Two minutes to go

"Two minutes to go . . . ease the genoa . . . ease the main . . . coming up, coming up . . . how far from the line?"

"Fifty yards."

"One-thirty to go," says the navigator.

"OK — power on the main, bring in the genoa, bearing away . . . "

"One minute."

"*****! Too early . . . dump the main . . . luffing . . . right, bearing away again . . . "

"Thirty seconds."

"Trim the main, trim the genoa . . . going for it. Don't oversheet the genoa, I want speed."

"Fifteen seconds — seen the boat to leeward?"

"Yes — we'll roll over him."

"Five, four, three, two, one, *gun*. Second gun — recall — don't think it was us."

"We're OK," calls the bowman. "A good half-a-length off it; 2468 and 700 were over. 2468's turning back."

The race is under way

And so the race is under way, with our yacht tolerably well away, but too close to that boat to leeward. There is space to tack, so we do. Now we are on port, crossing most of them: a bigger boat which started further up the line crosses ahead and a yellow boat, smoking along on starboard, looks set to cut us in half.

"Ready about — make it a good one! Ready? Go."

Our yacht slides neatly into and through her tack: on the yellow boat, close up on the weather quarter, the genoa backfills slightly and the helmsman bears away to the apparent header. Her crew are lined along the weather rail — hear no evil, speak no evil and see nothing at all — and it is only when she has to bear away even more for another 'header' that her helmsman sees our bow emerge from behind his forestay.

"Quick, tack," he yells and shoves the helm down. The crew scramble across the deck, the genoa catches briefly aback and the yacht stumbles round on to the other tack, her speed tumbling from five knots plus to one-and-a-half.

Clear air

Clear air now, and we can settle down for some fast sailing. The helmsman, no longer intent on squeezing up on the yacht to weather, eases off a fraction.

"Coming off a bit . . . there. On . . . on . . . on . . . "

As he calls his course, the genoa trimmer eases the sheet to keep the telltales streaming, the main trimmer lets the traveller a fraction down the track.

"Up point one . . . speed up point two . . . steady at five point five." reports the navigator.

Throughout the race, trimmer and helmsman keep up a constant conversation, so that the response to changes in the wind strength and direction are coordinated.

Others play their part in this segment of the race: the navigator monitors the course made good and the true strength and direction of the wind, either by calculation or by direct observation, using electronic instruments and performance computer.

"Headed another five — that's ten degrees since we tacked. I think we should go back — this won't be the paying tack any more."

"But I want to be over on this side of the course — there's less stream and I don't want to get too far away from 'Puppeteer' and 'Bandit'."

"OK, hold on — but if it breaks any more we have to go."

Up on the rail, there is more to do than simply make sure everyone's boots match: with the helmsman steering from leeward he cannot see over the weather rail, so a crew member keeps watch for the darkening of the water which indicates a gust.

"Puff coming — twenty seconds . . . ten . . . here it is."

The yacht heels more; and the genoa luff lifts as the puff also slightly heads.

"Main going down," as the mainsheet is eased down the traveller.

"Sheet coming in."

"Bearing away."

"Sheet going out."

"Coming back up" — and the interplay goes on.

Rounding the first mark

Unlike dinghy races, only a minority of races for yachts are sailed on perfect triangular courses. Most courses use natural obstacles or existing navigation marks as turning points.

Smart work with the nav computer shows that the next leg will be a shy reach, too shy for the spinnaker, so the high-clewed reacher comes up on deck. The genoa is up on the port halyard, in the port groove, so with the yacht on starboard tack the foredeck crew quickly flake the reacher along the starboard rail, hook on the tack and feed the head into the starboard feeder, then put a couple of sail ties round both sail and guardrail. The yacht tacks for the mark, and now the sail is in the right place, to leeward of the genoa but already bent on and ready to hoist.

On that yellow boat the crew have left the preparations too late. Although she too has tacked for the mark, two of them are still sliding around the foredeck, getting their feet wet and upsetting the genoa while they try to bundle the reacher under the skirt of the genoa and feed the head into the starboard groove which is now to leeward and outside the genoa. If they are not careful, the foaming bow wave will catch the unattached reacher and wash it aft, to trail like a drogue from out between the stanchions. There it goes . . .

Getting ready for the next reach

Well round the first mark now but it is only a short leg to the next mark, which has to be left to starboard: from there it is going to be a broad reach on starboard, so that means a gybe-set at the coming mark.

The .75 triradial is brought on deck and taken to

the rail, port side. In the cockpit, the sheets and guys are taken off their stowage cleats, and up forward are clipped to the sail. Happily, the foredeck hand had clipped both sets to the same stowage eye, even more happily to the port stowage eye, so there is no need to sit in the pulpit or struggle the lines round the front of the reacher. The port spinnaker halyard is brought to the rail by the sail, and clipped there — not yet to the sail in case, untended, its weight pulls the head of the sail out of the bag.

Now the pole is unshipped from its stowage along the starboard side of the foredeck. The starboard-side guy is put through the pole end and the topping lift clipped on, the forward end of the pole pushed under the genoa and into the pulpit and then the aft end lifted and fitted into the mast cup.

A final check on all the leads and the halyard is clipped on. The yacht rushes towards the mark. The helmsman bears away round the mark . . . the main trimmer hauls on the sheet, the boom comes to the centreline, gybes and the traveller crashes across the track — the (expletive deleted) traveller car should have been centred, and wasn't. Fortunately, no one's hand was in the way.

The reacher sheet is eased and taken on the other side, on the secondary winch. On the starboard side it is thrown right off the winch and the spinnaker guy swiftly loaded on while the foredeck hand lifts the end of the pole. In the cockpit the mainsheet hand, sheet cleated, overhauls the slack on the topping lift as the winch rings and, with the weight of the pole held by the topping lift, drops the line into the cam cleat. The foredeck hand runs to the mast and flings himself on the halyard. "Wrong one, Brian — the port halyard, you fool!"

The correct halyard is hauled hand over hand while at the winch the tailer overhauls the slack. Simultaneously in the cockpit the guy is being hauled aft on its winch and two turns of the spinnaker sheet have been thrown on to the port primary but plenty of slack left. The spinnaker blossoms out, flagging briefly while another turn is thrown on to the halyard winch and the handle fitted so the last eighteen inches of halyard can be wound up.

The spinnaker sheet is trimmed while the halyard winch hand, having secured the spinnaker halyard, moves to the reacher halyard and lets it go as the foredeck hand, moving forward again from the mast, catches the sail and hands it down on to the deck.

The helmsman settles on the course which the navigator had whispered in his ear just as they approached the mark and the trimmers set about settling the sail down. Pole aft, ease the sheet, up on the topping lift . . . raise the inboard end of the pole . . . take up the slack on the foreguy . . .

Changing the spinnaker

The wind has gradually lightened and drawn aft and this is now definitely the wrong sail: we should be using the half-ounce radial head. Time for a peel. With the triradial up on the port halyard, we must use the starboard halyard for the radial head and this gives us inside hoist/outside drop.

The sail is brought up and the clip on the bottom of the turtle hooked to the eye at the base of the aft, leeward leg of the pulpit. The lazy guy is transferred direct to the clew of the existing spinnaker. The sheet trimmer loads the lazy guy onto the secondary winch and transfers the weight of the sail to it, throwing the now slack sheet off the winch: the foredeck hand, moving to the lee shrouds, grabs the slack bight of the sheet and walks it forward until, briefly hauling the clew of the sail inboard by hand, he reaches up and trips the sheet clip from the sail. He clips the sheet to the clew of the new spinnaker, checking to see the lead is outside everything. He leads the starboard spinnaker halyard forward and round the forestay, back to the sail where he clips it on. He clips the peeling strop to the tack of the sail, and makes the loose end fast round the base of the forestay with a rolling hitch, adjusting the length so that the tack of the sail, with the strop pulled taut, is just above the top of the pulpit.

Up goes the halyard as the sheet is trimmed and the new sail sets, somewhat imperfectly, inside the triradial. The pole goes forward, the triradial is tripped, the guy clipped to the new sail, the peeling strop tripped, the pole comes aft and the foredeck hand moves aft to join the hand already gathering the triradial.

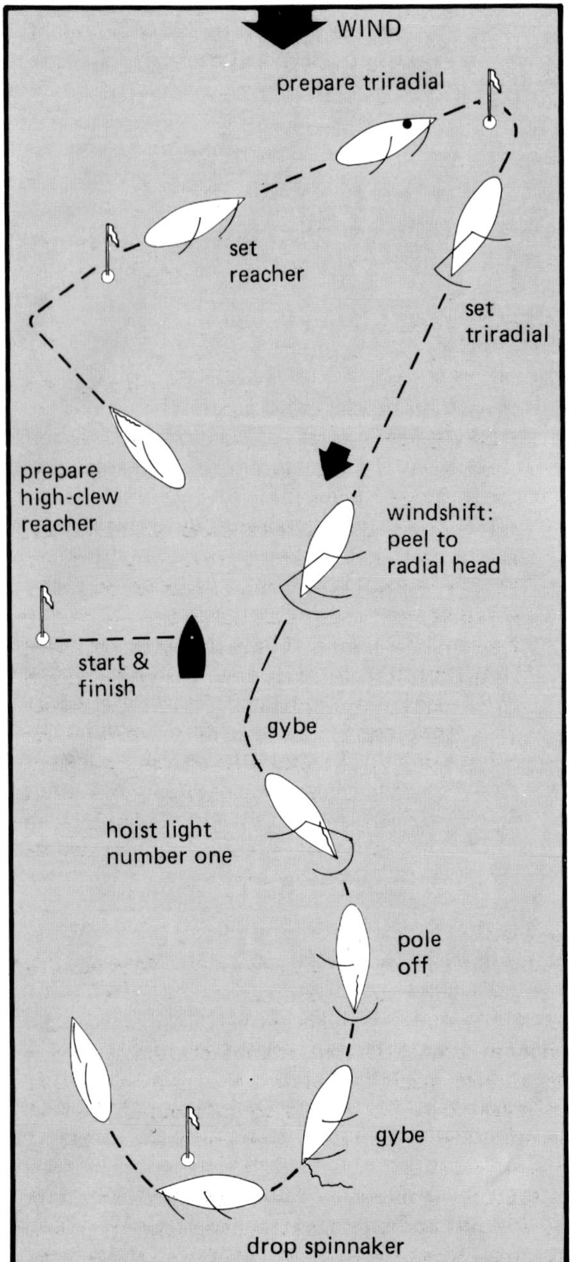

It all goes so smoothly that on the yellow boat, now a little way astern, they don't even notice that we have peeled. Our speed, which had been dropping each time our triradial dropped, steadies and then, as the lighter and fuller radial-head spinnaker continues to float high and free above us, slowly creeps back up.

The wind continues to veer until, not far short of the mark, we have to slip in a gybe — smooth enough, but now we will have to gybe again as we round the mark for the beat back home.

The high-clewed reacher is cleared up from where we dumped it and packed away, and the light number one comes up to take its place. With only a little way to go to the mark, we prepare it on the port side, where we'll need it after the gybe back, rather than on the starboard side where it properly should go. Up it goes, on the port genoa halyard but with the tack taken right forward so that it does not interfere with the still-flying spinnaker.

Coming into the mark, off comes the pole while the spinnaker looks after itself, floating high and setting even better while square running like this without the overshort pole the rating rule requires us to use.

With the pole stowed, the yacht begins her gybe, only a length or two short of the mark now. As the main boom crosses the centreline and the genoa trimmer brings home the genoa sheet, the port spinnaker sheet and guy are allowed to run. The foredeck hand, with a back-up, has the starboard lazy guy in hand on the foredeck and swiftly hauls the tack of the sail down to the deck, even as the sail begins to flag out ahead of the forestay. Swiftly they start gathering the sail as the halyard is let go, and as the yacht neatly hardens up round the mark the sail flutters down onto the foredeck.

On that yellow boat, when they eventually reach the mark, they will probably take the spinnaker off before gybing, and take even longer to complete the last length or two into the mark in the failing afternoon breeze.

Meanwhile, our own yacht settles down for the final beat home, watching the windshifts and the telltales . . .

13 · Living on board

As soon as you arrive on board, find out where you can stow your gear. You will most probably be given a locker of your own, and it should be a point of pride with you that all your gear — boots and oilskins, which have their own stowage, excepted — is either in there or on you. Your watch and sunglasses, contact lens case and personalised sweatband will not please the navigator when they turn up on the chart table.

What to take

How much you take depends on how big the boat is and how long the race is going to be. Aim to take with you as little as possible, but at the same time do not go without something you need. The crew member who turns up with just boots and one light bag is always welcome, but the person who has to keep borrowing sweaters, towels and someone else's oilskin is just a nuisance. The crew member who gets wet and cold in the first two hours because he or she has not the proper clothing is a liability.

Some skippers may well tell you exactly what to bring, and exactly what you will be provided with on board: others may say "whatever you like, as long as it's only in one bag" while the fanatical may give you a maximum weight of gear you can bring. Always take:

- oilskins
- boots
- the clothes you stand up in, plus one layer (it is always colder on the water than on the land).

For more than a day race, add:

- a change of clothes, from the skin out;
- two towels, one big one, and one for round the neck;
- enough personal hygiene equipment to make your proximity bearable by those around you (it can be truly awful sharing the rail with someone who hasn't brushed their teeth for four days);
- shore-going clothes, if needed.

You should check:

- whether bedding is provided, or whether you bring your own sleeping bag;
- whether safety harnesses are provided, or whether you bring your own (and then bring your own anyway);
- whether you should bring shore-going clothes, and if so the standard of dress expected. Although many yacht clubs are informal, the owner may not wish his boat to be represented ashore by a bunch of ruffians who look as if they own only one pair of jeans each, none less than eight years old. In addition, the owner and other crew members may want to eat ashore in a good restaurant or a more formal club: for many of us, offshore racing is a social as well as a sporting pastime, and you don't want to miss the party just because you are the only one who did not bring a tie.

Clothing

A T-shirt and a pair of jeans, sweaters added according to environment, is still basic working wear for most offshore sailors, and is entirely adequate for the occasional crew. Several manufacturers however now produce specialised clothing, usually as part of an integrated system with a trade name like Warm Wear or Polar Wear, which crew who sail a lot find it worthwhile to buy.

A typical complete outfit might thus consist of long-sleeved undervest, with long-legged pants, worn next the skin but over such personal underwear as you normally wear; a lightweight roll-neck sweater; a sleeveless, longlegged quilted garment; a quilted jacket. On top of this is worn oilskin trousers and jacket, with thick warm socks on the feet and boots.

This outfit is very warm — too warm for an inshore race on a sunny day — but the system is designed so that bits such as the long underwear can be left off when necessary. The advantage of such an outfit is its comfort and suitability — it is designed after all for offshore sailing — coupled with lightness and lack of bulk. Wearing such an outfit, only three layers are required and the modern materials of which this thermal clothing is made are very light: thus easy to stow and carry.

One disadvantage is that it is a curious-looking outfit in which to walk up the High Street of the town that the race visits, and will draw even more curious glances on the train coming home after the race; so normal shoreside clothes, albeit jeans and sweater, must be taken as well, unless the boat is going out only to race.

Oilskins

For day sailing, a simple anorak and waterproof trousers will usually be enough to keep out the worst of the wet, but for longer races or sailing at night, something more substantial is needed. A good suit of offshore oilskins has:

- chest-high trousers, combined with a zip-up jacket;
- jacket and trousers that are lined, loosely, with a lightweight waterproof material that cuts down condensation inside the suit, and adds a measure of thermal insulation;
- all the seams of both garments welded or glued and taped, to keep them waterproof;
- cuffs on trousers and jacket with some sort of seal, for when it's really wet;
- jacket with some sort of integral buoyancy, even if it's only a lining of closed-cell foam;
- a jacket with a high, stand-up collar which will protect the ears, with a tuck-away hood for when it is raining or really cold;
- a safety harness built in to the jacket probably with closable pockets to stow the buckles when not in use;
- a whistle on a lanyard stitched into one jacket pocket, for use as an emergency locator if you go overboard.

Additional features might include an inflatable collar, possibly with a small gas bottle; light-reflecting tape on the front, at the wrists (to be seen when waving) and on the back of the collar, to help find you in the dark if you go overboard; 'hand-warmer' pockets under the main pockets; two-way zips to allow you to get into certain areas of the suit without doing a mid-ocean strip act.

If you intend sailing more than once or twice a season, one of these suits is a worthwhile investment.

Safety

While this book was in preparation, one of Britain's best-known and respected racing seamen lost his life through falling overboard two miles from harbour on a routine delivery voyage. It was a salutary reminder to everyone that accidents do happen and that safety systems can fail.

Non-sailors place much emphasis on the wearing of lifejackets while afloat, but it is worth remembering that a lifejacket is utterly useless, save as a pillow, on a yacht. Off the yacht, its worth increases dramatically but it is always much better to stay on the yacht in the first place.

There should be a safety harness on board for every crew member, and before each race each crew member — the newcomer especially — should find his or her safety harness, put it on and adjust the fit: not so tight that it restricts breathing, but tight enough to hold the wearer securely. Put the harness on and then imagine yourself going over the side, with only the tether between you and death. Is the chest strap so loose that as soon as the tether jerks taut, inevitably from a point above your head, the buckle is jerked upwards and hits you in the teeth? Rendered thus unconscious, your arms hanging limp, will the harness just pull off over your head?

For this reason, most serious crew have their own harness, clearly marked with name and adjusted to fit. Best of all, perhaps, is a harness built into your

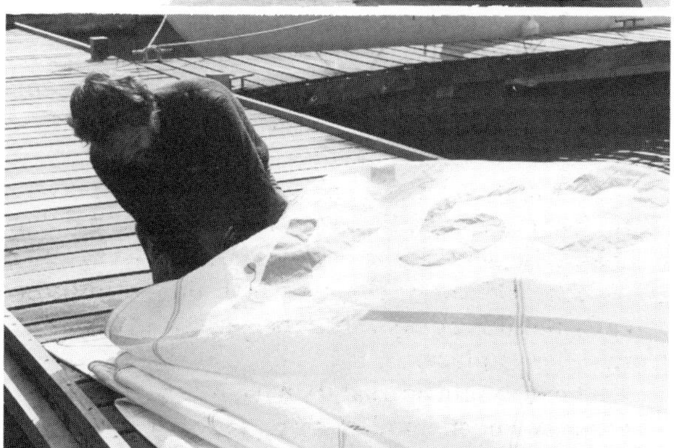

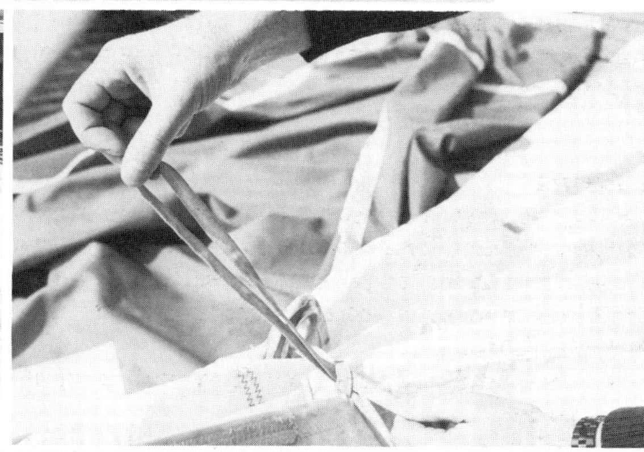

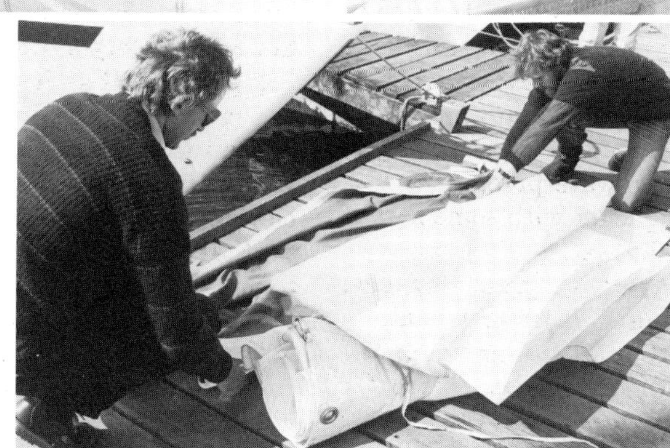

ABOVE *Folding a headsail ashore.*

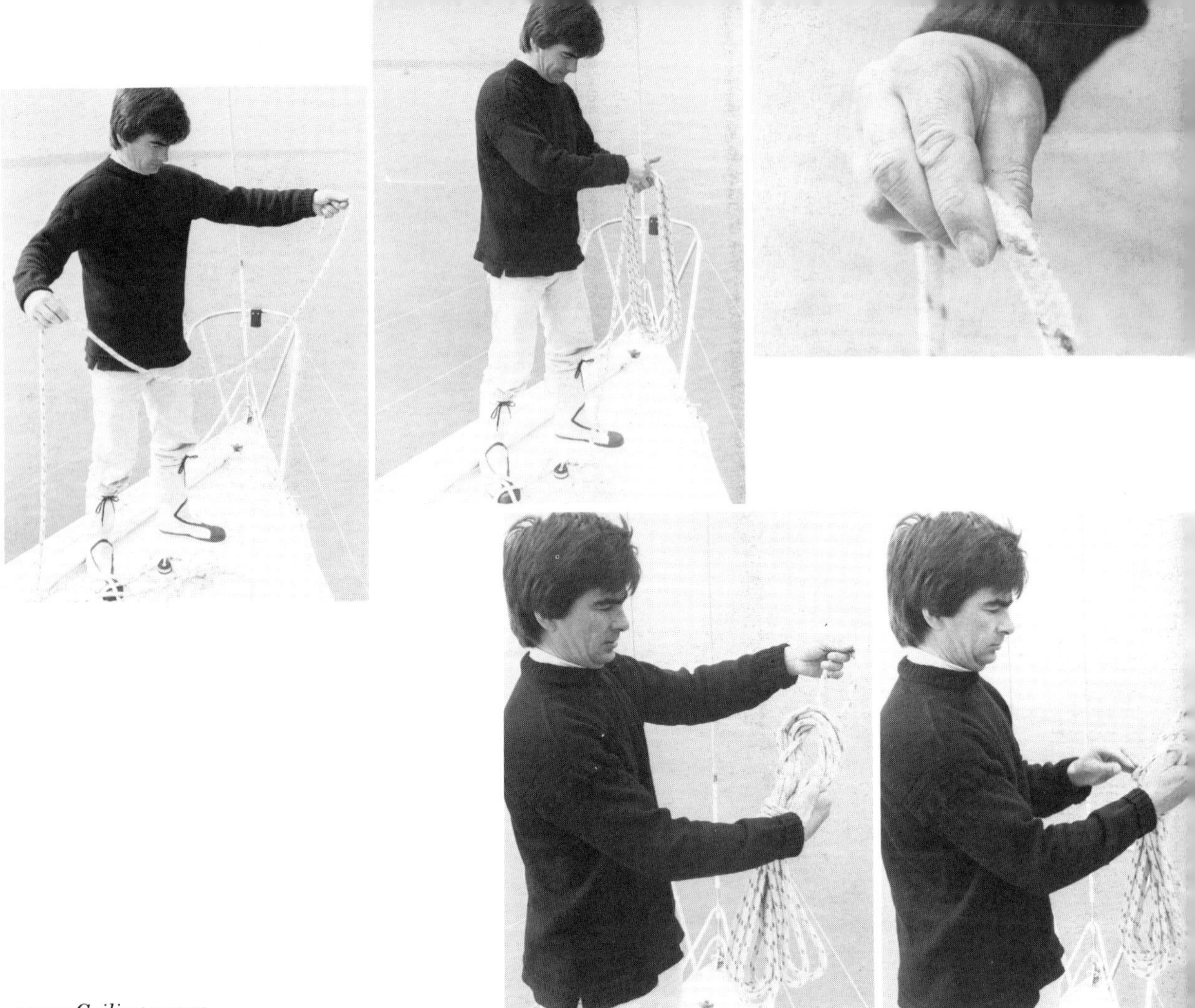

ABOVE Coiling a rope.

jacket — but there are times, in warm weather at night for example, when you might want a harness but not the jacket. In European or North American waters at least, such moments are rare.

Sea sickness

Sea sickness affects, to a greater or lesser degree, nearly all those who race offshore, and it particularly affects the inexperienced. Do not be afraid to bring your own favourite remedy with you, or to find out what other people take. In addition, some simple precautions will reduce the chances of being sick:

- take no alcohol for at least 24 hours before the race;
- Avoid greasy or exotic foods for at least 24 hours before the race;
- get a good night's sleep before the race;
- do not let yourself get cold and wet on the race.

There is, however, only one infallible cure for sea sickness: sit under an apple tree for half-an-hour.

Watch systems

Traditionally, the crew of a sailing vessel is divided into sections called watches, each in the charge of a

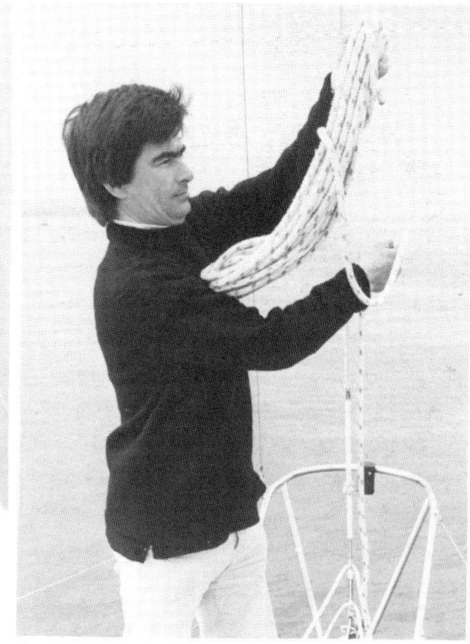

mate and each coming on duty at set times of the day. The usual length of a watch at sea is four hours, and in, for example, the British naval system two two-hour watches (the Dog Watches) in the afternoon ensure a rotation so that all watches take an equal share of night and day, light and darkness.

This system, so admirable for running a vessel with a regular routine and a long voyage ahead of her, has proven to be one of the least efficient ways of running a racing yacht, but the traditions of the sea die hard and many yachts, especially those with 'old and bold' owners, stick to it.

If two watches are to be used, three hours is plenty long enough at night for a nine-to-five human fresh — or rather jaded — from a week in the office, while few races are long enough to let the crew settle comfortably into a proper watch routine.

Most successful boats now use a rolling watch system, where each member of the crew goes off or comes on at a different time to all the others, whilst if the crew is large enough (six or more) the skipper and the navigator do not take regular watches, but are on call, if not on deck, all the time.

In a six-person crew, it works like this: 1 and 2 are

skipper and navigator, and outside the watch routine. They arrange between themselves to cover for each other when one is below. The remaining crew, 3, 4, 5 and 6, have a basic watch of two hours on deck, one hour sheltering below but on immediate call — that means fully clad but cat-napping — and one hour off watch, sleeping.

So we start the race with everyone on deck and having a great time racing the boat. As night comes on, but before exhaustion from the hard day at the office overtakes everyone, we start the watches. Crew members 3 and 6 stay on watch, 4 and 5 go below with 5 remaining on call. An hour later 4 comes back on, 6 goes on call and 5 stays below for an hour's more kip. An hour later 3 goes on call, 5 comes up and 6 goes off. An hour later, 6 comes back on deck and 5 goes below on call, and so on.

In this example it is assumed that everyone is equally good at all tasks, including steering and that either the navigator or skipper is always up and about. One hour may not sound much for sleep, but with the system running it is really two hours (with perhaps an interruption in the first) and this is adequate over a short race. Over longer races skipper and navigator would have to come into the rota to give longer breaks, or with more people on board longer breaks would occur naturally.

The advantage of the rolling system is that it avoids that awful hour when those on deck are watching the clock instead of the sails, and it avoids the break in continuity that occurs when there is a complete crew change at the change of watch. With the rolling system there is always someone fresh in their first hour on deck, and yet someone who has been on deck long enough to keep track of what is going on outside the guardrails.

Being asked back

Racing regularly on big boats is a very satisfying hobby, and becoming a reliable and valuable crew member is the easiest way for most of us to enjoy this hobby: owning big boats is an expensive pastime, and for most of us owning and campaigning a racing boat of over, say, 33 ft is just a dream.

The very big boats, and the top racing boats, are in the main crewed by young men who are professionals in all but name: employed by sailmakers, sparmakers or others in the business — or occasionally in one of the owner's companies — they race boats as part and parcel of their job, and to compete for places with these full-time experts the true amateur has to be very good, very dedicated and have plenty of free time.

This, however, is only the highly visible tip of the offshore racing iceberg. Most yachts outside the handful of true international racers are crewed by amateurs: once into the racing scene and tolerably competent, good crews should have no trouble finding a boat which is good fun to race in, where the lifestyle afloat and ashore suits their tastes and pocket and where they can become a member of a happy team.

There are as many ways of running a boat as there are owners and it is impossible to give hard and fast rules about who pays for what or who does what. On larger boats, especially those at the sharp end of the racing, it is normal for the owner to pay for just about everything, perhaps even providing oilskins and some clothing for the regular crew, especially if 'team colours' are worn. On such yachts food and drink (quite a few serious boats are alcohol-free zones, but the crew make up for it ashore) are normally provided, but it is reasonable on boats on a less lavish budget for the crew to pay a share of the direct costs — food, drink, entry fees — of the race. Many smaller yachts run on a co-operative basis, where the regular crew pay a contribution to the yacht's upkeep, but for this they have in return a greater say in the yacht's programme and may have the use of the boat at times when she is not racing.

23456789